IMAGES
of America

LAKE CHAMPLAIN
ISLANDS

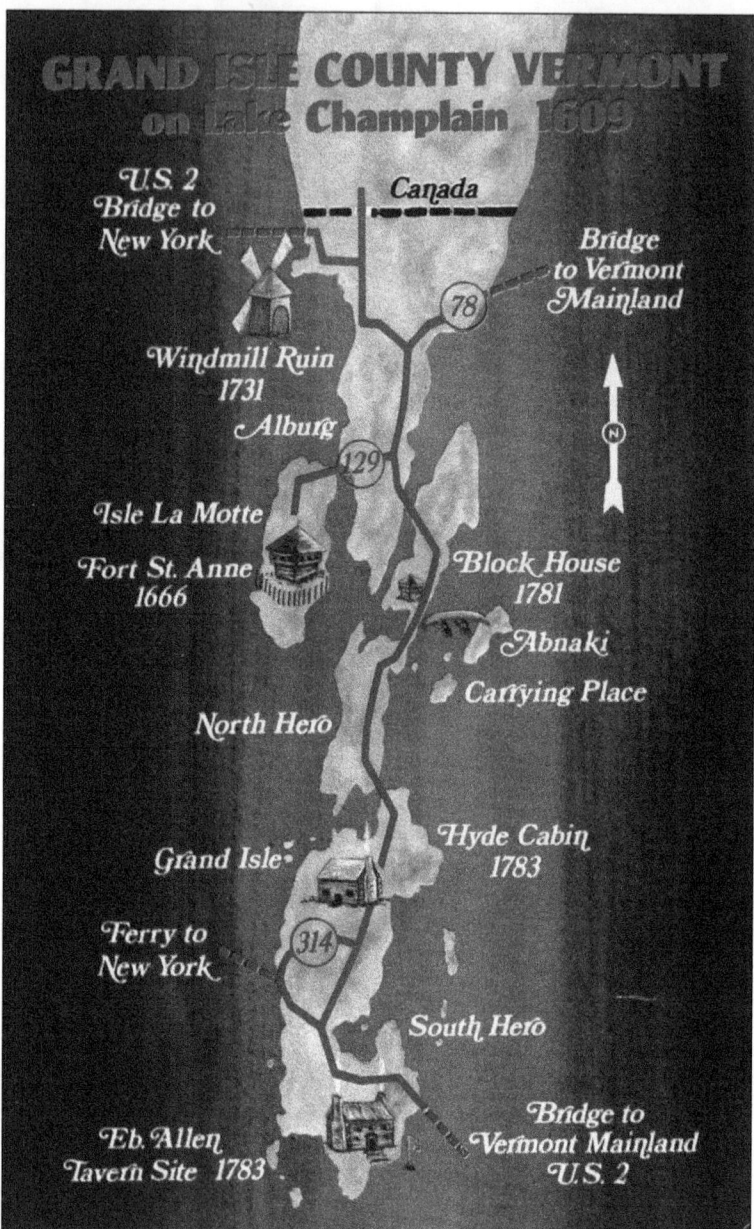

All five Champlain Island towns are depicted in this 1960s map. British sympathizers during the Revolutionary War settled in Alburgh. Isle La Motte was named for Captain de la Motte who constructed Fort St. Anne. The two "hero" islands were claimed by brothers Ethan and Ira Allen. Grand Isle was considered part of South Hero and became Middle Hero in 1798, then Grand Isle in 1910. (Courtesy of Tracy Giroux.)

On the cover: Edward Duba and Andrew L. Holcomb display the results of a successful fishing expedition on Lake Champlain. This photograph, taken in the late 1800s, marks a day after Holcomb had returned from a lengthy absence from the islands after working as a field engineer designing and building jails in Texas. (Courtesy of the Isle La Motte Historical Society.)

IMAGES
of America

LAKE CHAMPLAIN
ISLANDS

Tara Liloia

ARCADIA
PUBLISHING

Published by Arcadia Publishing
Charleston, South Carolina

Library of Congress Catalog Card Number: 2008934835

For all general information contact Arcadia Publishing at:
Telephone 843-853-2070
Fax 843-853-0044
E-mail sales@arcadiapublishing.com
For customer service and orders:
Toll-Free 1-888-313-2665

Visit us on the Internet at www.arcadiapublishing.com

To Dave and Trevor, for everything they do.

CONTENTS

ACKNOWLEDGMENTS

I would like to offer my heartfelt thanks to all the Vermont and Grand Isle County historical societies and museums that opened their collections for this book: Robert and Gloria McEwen and the Isle La Motte Historical Society, Tracy Giroux and the North Hero Historical Society, Chris and Howy Tepper and the Alburgh Historical Society, Jan DeSarno and the Grand Isle Historical Society, Nancy Allen and the board of the South Hero Museum, and Christie Carter at the Vermont State Archives. I also would like to express my appreciation to all the individual collectors who offered unfettered access to their archival photograph and artifact collections: Ron Fierstein, Scott Newman, Selby and Maureen Turner, Marty Dale, Gail and Ken Yocis, Betty and Robert Pike, Rachelle Quiser, Norma Wales, Susan McBride Crowley, Robin Gutierrez, and Ann Wetzel. Without your generous assistance, this book would not have come to be.

INTRODUCTION

As we round the corner toward the 400th anniversary of Samuel de Champlain's arrival in Vermont, it feels appropriate to look back at the events, people, and places that brought us to this point in time. Our islands have existed as towns since before America was a nation itself. We live with the ancient record of our past on a daily basis in our stone buildings, on our dirt roads, and in the fossils buried within the islands themselves.

In our earliest days, there are no records of European exploration throughout the islands in Lake Champlain. Not until Samuel de Champlain wrote a journal of his 1609 trip down the Richelieu River did we have a written account of settlers here. Even then, it took nearly 60 years for the French to make their way back to the lake permanently after Champlain continued his travels elsewhere. It is certain that French settlers encountered Native Americans, some friendly, some not, during their return in the late 1600s. Fort St. Anne, constructed on the shores of Isle La Motte, is evidence of the attempt to shield the outpost from Iroquois attacks.

As skirmishes with the local tribes continued, the King of France granted the islands to land developers in exchange for faithful allegiance to the crown. Any Frenchman living there would have to pledge himself, and surely some of his profits, to the nation of France. Some of the Lake Champlain towns were given to various grantees, most of whom failed to build up their domain and subsequently lost rights to them. In a clever law, the British declared that the land was theirs and only French settlers in the area who had actually improved their land could retain it. In one fell swoop, most of the islands became British owned in 1768 through this decree. In addition, those parcels that were occupied were soon purchased by eager British land speculators from French settlers eager to exit the new British territory.

After the Revolutionary War, Vermont petitioned the Continental Congress to become the 14th state, but it was denied admission to the new union. Not a group known to sit idly by and accept such a decision, Vermont's leadership wrote its own constitution in 1777 and announced the birth of the Republic of Vermont. This declaration of independence revoked all previous claims on the land, including those in the Lake Champlain Islands and added to an already-intricate system of land rights in the area. We find an example of this in Alburgh, where the land was leased from Britain to Canadian Col. Henry Caldwell. British loyalists fleeing revolutionary persecution in other states found sanctuary in the town, believing it to be fundamentally British land. They found themselves in quite a quandary when the peninsula passed from French to British and then to American hands. Skirmishes between landowners and passing soldiers were not uncommon during this time.

In the lower islands, as soon as the new Vermont government began to grant charters, Ethan Allen and three of his associates petitioned for rights to the "two heroes," now known as North

Hero, Grand Isle, and South Hero. We can look back and chuckle at the modesty of brothers Ethan and Ira Allen, who named the islands after themselves. Their request was granted by Gov. Thomas Chittenden, the land was divided into parcels, and the first settlers began to arrive around 1783. As families arrived and disputes arose, the need for government spurred the creation of a county court in North Hero and the establishment of town meetings.

From 1791 until 1860, the population of the islands boomed from 1,292 to 4,276 people, creating a critical need for transportation, lodging, skilled tradesmen, and merchants. This commercial era was brought about by the rise of the steamboat and the establishment of permanent roads and led the way for the railroad expansion to come. Many of the buildings and shops built in this era were made with posterity in mind and are still in use today. Often just a glance above the door of a local library or general store will tell you that it has been in operation since this thriving period in time.

After the prosperous 19th century, the character of the islands changed yet again. Tourism became a primary source of income as the working class found enough leisure time to relax on our beaches and swim in our chilly waters. Large boardinghouses providing rooms and meals gave way to smaller cabins and casual snack shops. Commercial farms, which had worked to bring milk, butter, and apples the masses in Boston and New York, began to cater to locals with high-quality products and hands-on recreational experiences.

Our area is so rich in folklore and history that one could write six volumes on the subject and still not complete the work. Indeed, just 20 years ago, Allen Stratton took on that monumental task and left us with an encyclopedia of Lake Champlain history that remains unrivaled to this day. Instead of a futile attempt to compete with his work, I have attempted to draw upon his knowledge to tell the stories of the islands in images and bring the history that he left off two decades ago into the modern age.

Residents, you should be proud of your islands and the resilient spirit that keeps your communities humming after ice storms, tornadoes, and other challenges. It is the kind of place where residents shrug off two weeks without power with a casual, "at least we could bathe in the lake." And it is the kind of place where you will not have a flat tire five minutes before someone will pull up to give you a hand.

I had the honor of accompanying my neighbors out onto the lake to meet the replica schooner *Lois McClure* on her journey southward toward Burlington. Aside from the majesty of the ship's lines, I was amazed at what I saw. As the boat pulled away from the dock, traces of modernity faded into invisibility. Gone were the power lines, paved roads, and automobiles. Just a short distance from the shoreline, I was able to see what Samuel de Champlain saw: several fine islands with thick trees packed so tightly that only a stripe of rocky shoreline was visible beneath them. They are a special place, full of character, community, and promise.

One

EARLY EXPLORATION
SAMUEL DE CHAMPLAIN

Lake Champlain takes its name from French explorer Samuel de Champlain. After founding Quebec City in Canada, Champlain sailed south down the Richelieu River with two of his crew and about 60 Algonquin and Montagnais natives. The explorers encountered a group of hostile Iroquois, who retreated after Champlain felled two of their chiefs with one shot of his arquebus. (Courtesy of the Isle La Motte Historical Society.)

Samuel de Champlain landed his canoe on the northern tip of Isle La Motte in July 1609 accompanied by a group of Native Americans from several tribes. Champlain declared that he had found "four fine islands, ten, twelve and fifteen leagues long." A statue honoring Champlain was dedicated at his original landing place in 1968. (Courtesy of the Isle La Motte Historical Society.)

Recently scholars have debunked claims that widely circulated portraits (often attributed to an image created by Louis Cesar Joseph Ducornet) of Champlain accurately portray the Frenchman. This drawing, done as a self-portrait by Champlain himself, is now considered one of only two historically accurate depictions of the explorer. (Courtesy of the Isle La Motte Historical Society.)

Two

DAILY LIFE
SCHOOLS, CHURCHES,
AND COMMUNITY

North Hero Community Hall, also known as the town hall, was used for town meetings, social events, the office of the town clerk, and the local library. Funding for construction was raised by the North Hero Community Club in 1929. The building is now in the hands of the North Hero Historical Society, which intends to restore it as a community hall once again. (Courtesy of Tracy Giroux.)

L. and L. Motte Home was established as a home for destitute children in 1892 in accordance with the will of Lewis and Laura Motte. The home was in operation for over 85 years. Up to 10 children (aged 7–18) at a time were given housing, food, clothing, and education. The building still exists on South Hero as the Apple Island Campground and Marina. (Courtesy of the South Hero Museum.)

Eleven-year-old Susan McBride was a contestant in the 1948 Vermont 4-H Dress Review as a member of Polly's Sewers of South Hero. Participants were required to create a dress as well as select or make accessories like shoes, hats, and purses. In their record books, girls noted the cost of all raw materials that went into the creation of their dresses. (Courtesy of Susan McBride Crowley.)

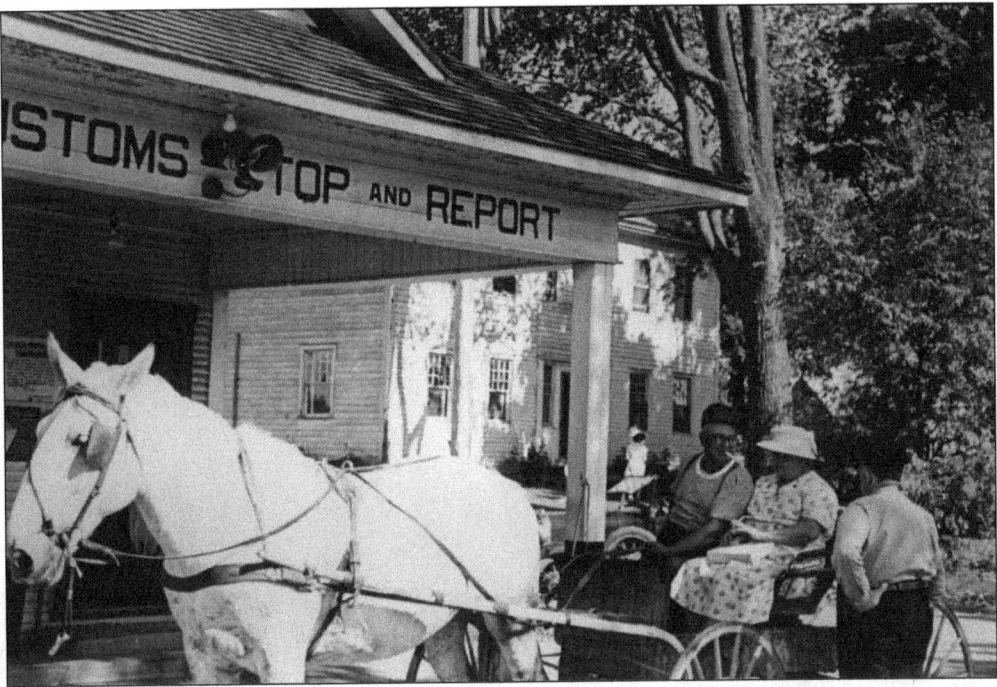

By 1937, construction had been completed the bridge between Alburgh and Rouses Point, New York. This couple stops to check in with border guards and pay the toll before continuing on to Alburgh. This tollbooth was in operation until the mid-1970s, until it was shut down due to structural damage. (Courtesy of the Vermont State Archives and Records Administration.)

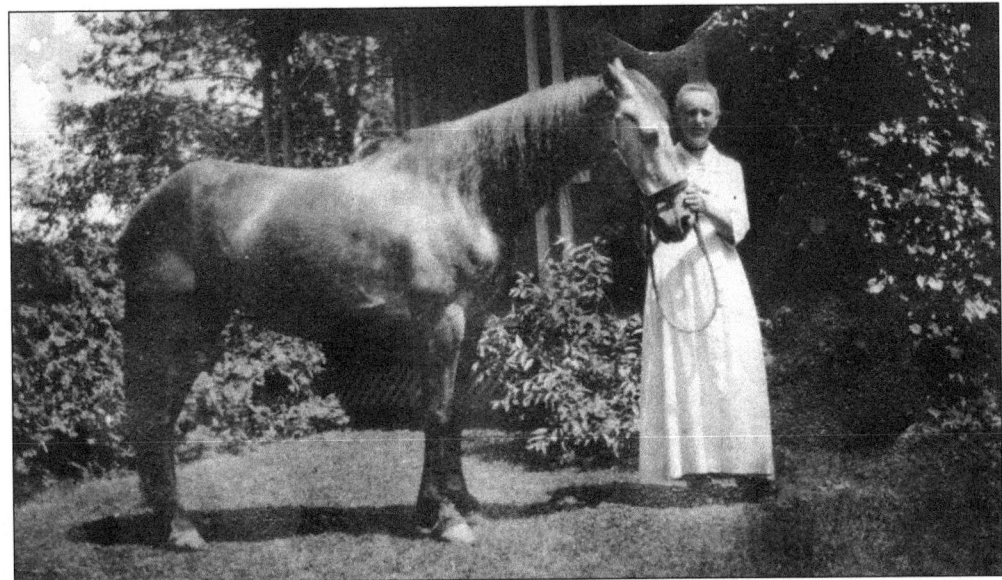

The Landon Memorial Building in South Hero was donated to the town by Susan (Hall) Landon in 1924 in memory of her son Arthur who died of influenza in France in 1919, following a tour of duty in World War I. The building served as town library until recent years. It now houses the South Hero Museum. (Courtesy of the South Hero Museum.)

PUBLIC LIBRARY, ISLE LA MOTT VT. 138.

The Isle La Motte Library Association was formed in 1868, but it was not until 30 years later that the group was able to acquire 120 books from the State of Vermont to round out its collection. The present home of the library was built by Ira Hill in 1830 and eventually sold to Nelson Fisk and used as a tenant home until 1904. When Fisk posted the building for sale, the library association asked him to hold the stone house for them until they were able to raise enough funds for the purchase. Money for the project was so scarce that when purchasing the current building, the ladies of the library took out personal loans to complete the $500 sale. Cynthia Ritchie, then 12 years old, offered to become the town librarian in 1898. She held the position for 64 years until her retirement in 1962 and received a commendation from the governor of Vermont for her role as the longest-serving librarian in the state. (Courtesy of the Isle La Motte Historical Society.)

A library has been present in Alburgh since the earliest records in 1882. In January 1928, the library building caught fire and quick-thinking librarians threw the books into the snow toward safety from the flames. Unfortunately, the librarians then had to wipe the icy coating off the individual pages in a freezing basement, lest the snow melt and cause water damage to the books. Paul Pearl also lost his flagship department store in Alburgh to fire in May 1944, the ruins of which can be seen above and below. Instead of rebuilding his store, Pearl donated his lot to the Alburgh Library Association, which worked with the town to create a combination library and municipal building that opened to the public in 1962. (Courtesy of the Alburgh Historical Society.)

In the early 19th century, a schoolhouse was built in northern Isle La Motte to accommodate children who could not reach the south district through the impassable marsh. This school was located about a mile north of the town center. Later locations included the Methodist church basement (1856), the second floor of town hall (1914), and a dedicated building on School Street (1930). (Courtesy of the Isle La Motte Historical Society.)

Families paid tuition for each child who attended classes and were also required to provide half a cord of firewood for heating the classroom. Often, parents fell behind on payments; in 1810, the north district was only able to collect $12.42 of the $200 owed to the school. Seen here, the south district school currently houses the town's historical society museum. (Author's collection.)

The Station School offered instruction for Alburgh children in grades one through eight (the fifth-grade class of 1935 is shown above) and was used until 1969 when elementary students from all the district schools were consolidated into the old Alburgh High School. The building is now known as the Islands in the Sun Senior Center. (Courtesy of the Alburgh Historical Society.)

Alburgh was originally divided into seven school districts when the first schools were chartered in 1803. Three more districts were added shortly thereafter, and teachers were hired after passing an examination in spelling, reading, writing, geography, and arithmetic. The Station School (here in 1941) was built in the village of Alburgh in 1905 to accommodate the population rise from the new railroad. (Courtesy of the Alburgh Historical Society.)

Construction on the Alburgh High School was started in August 1938 and cost the town and state $64,800. The building was dedicated in 1939 by Gov. George D. Aiken, as well as groups of younger children from the surrounding district schools. That first year's enrollment included 55 freshmen. The town also transferred 30 grammar school students from the seventh- and eighth-grade classes at the Station School (also referred to as the Village School), Bush School, and Bay District to the new high school. Some of those original students were part of the 1943 Alburgh High School graduating class, seen above. In the image below, the 1941 Alburgh junior class poses while other students look on from the windows. (Courtesy of the Alburgh Historical Society.)

Seen above, Shirley Mitchell rides her bicycle in front of the recently built high school building on Main Street in Alburgh. The new building included room for up to 150 students in five classrooms, as well as an auditorium with room for 400 people. In the image below, the auditorium has been decorated with streamers and a pair of "thrones" for the 1942 junior prom. The school served the community for 29 years until it was converted into a grammar school and the high school students were bused elsewhere. To this day, Champlain Island teenagers attend high school in neighboring mainland towns. (Courtesy of the Alburgh Historical Society.)

The Isle La Motte United Methodist Church building was started in 1843; however, limited funds stretched construction over a five-year period. The church was completed in 1848 and served the community until 1856, when a chimney fire took down everything but the walls. The town rallied and raised enough money to repair and rededicate the church in the same year. (Courtesy of the Isle La Motte Historical Society.)

Rev. Henry Taylor was appointed to lead Isle La Motte's Methodist community in 1847. Reverend Taylor nearly died one winter bringing back lumber pledged to the church after his boat capsized. After 11 hours in the icy water, he and his two companions managed to make land and survive. Here the parsonage is visible, built next to the church in 1874. (Author's collection.)

Catholic priests traveled from as far as Milton, Vermont, and Clarenceville, Canada, to serve the North Hero community until 1887 when St. Benedict's Church was opened. It originally had shoreline property where the North Hero House's Homestead building is currently located. It was moved in 1949 to a spot south of the village. The Homestead building rests on the church's abandoned Isle La Motte limestone foundation. (Courtesy of Tracy Giroux.)

The Catholic congregation in South Hero was constructing a new church building when the existing church was gutted by fire in July 1898. Devoted Fr. Joseph Turcotte nearly perished while attempting to save several holy items from the blaze. The new building was completed, and St. Rose of Lima provided meeting space for parishioners from as far away as Milton, Burlington, and Plattsburgh, New York. (Courtesy of the South Hero Museum.)

The chapel at St. Anne's Shrine in Isle La Motte was constructed in 1666 under the watchful eye of Father Dollier de Casson of Montreal. The fort was abandoned in 1670, and the sandy beachfront was popular with travelers. Little else is recorded from St. Anne's until over 200 years later. In 1892, the land where the fort and chapel once stood had become the property of Henry Hill. Burlington-based Bishop Louis DeGoesbriand purchased the parcel from Hill and built a sanctuary housing a statue of St. Anne and a 32-foot-high wooden cross. Later a dock was added to accommodate the numerous pilgrims who arrived at the shrine via steamer. (Courtesy of the Isle La Motte Historical Society.)

Alburgh, Isle La Motte, and North Hero made up one Catholic parish in 1886. Bishop Amedeus Rappe made frequent missions to Isle La Motte to say masses in private houses in the town. Indeed, it was noted that the island was his favorite destination. Bishop Rappe thought that the community was in need of its own church, and he generously offered the bulk of the funding from his own savings. (A Cleveland parishioner's donation of shares in a silver mine on Lake Superior had left Bishop Rappe in a fine financial position.) In 1871, the bishop purchased a half acre of land from Joseph Duba Sr. and built St. Joseph's church. This building (above) was used for 94 years until replaced in 1965. The new building is seen below, just after completion in 1966. (Courtesy of the Isle La Motte Historical Society.)

In 1903, the Episcopal Society decided to build a church in Alburgh with an estimated cost of just over $3,300. The town's ladies society collected nearly 30 percent of the necessary building funds from chicken pie suppers, a strawberry festival, and selling handmade goods. Mason and Company Builders completed the work in September 1905, and St. Luke's Episcopal Church (pictured in the 1940s) was opened. (Courtesy of the Alburgh Historical Society.)

The North Cemetery found near the Isle La Motte Corners was established in the early 1800s with the burial of Capt. Caleb Hill in 1814, whose marker reads "Shot by Soldiers from the U.S. Fleet." Gail Yocis is shown visiting the Jesse W. Holcomb headstone in August 1957. (Courtesy of Gail and Ken Yocis.)

Three

RECREATION
LAKE CHAMPLAIN

In the late 1800s, Lake Champlain entered its heyday as a recreational paradise. Steamers and railroads brought eager tourists to the islands for quiet reflection and outdoor activities. Tent camping on Lake Champlain was a refreshing prospect for those who came from the crowds of New York, Boston, or Montreal. The accommodations were not always rough—note the bed and sofa inside the tent. (Courtesy of Tracy Giroux.)

This Sunday afternoon game of croquet was played on the Holcomb lawn around 1898. Croquet was a popular family sport since the mid-1800s. The Holcomb family patriarch, Wyman, took this photograph of (from left to right) Wesley Miller, Evelyn Holcomb, Julia Holcomb and her son Ransom, Arthur Hill and an unidentified man, Lyndhurst Holcomb, and Emmett and Helen Vosburgh. (Courtesy of the Isle La Motte Historical Society.)

Bass fishing on Lake Champlain started in the late 18th century and experienced a surge in popularity over the last 50 years. Yet invasive fish and plants have begun to change the ecosystem in the lake, threatening the prospects of future fishermen. Eurasian milfoil, zebra mussels, and sea lamprey are some nonlocal flora and fauna that are dominating the native species in the lake. (Courtesy of Tracy Giroux.)

COMPANY "A" ETHAN ALLEN TRAINING CAMP, NO. HERO, VT. 53.

An April 1919 advertisement for the Ethan Allen Training Camp on North Hero declared that the camp "combines an ideal summer vacation. . . with Military and Physical Training by real West Pointers." For just $225 a term, boys ranging from age 14 through 21 were treated to fishing, boating, canoeing, hiking, games, and sports between their drills and exercises. Tuition covered an entire summer, from July 1 to September 1. In the photograph above, a uniformed Company A falls in line at the camp. Seen below, the semipermanent men's barracks overlooks Lake Champlain. (Above, courtesy of Ron Fierstein; below, courtesy of Tracy Giroux.)

THE CANTONMENT, ETHAN ALLEN TRAINING CAMP, NO. HERO, VT. 62.

PARKER HOUSE
NORTH HERO, VT.

In 1908, the Parker House (seen above) was run by owner John N. Parker (as well as his wife, Alvira McBride, until her death in 1904). This boardinghouse saw a great deal of traffic, the extent of which was noted in a July 18, 1895, newspaper item for North Hero: "John N. Parker's dock has become a necessity as the boat has occasion to stop every day and nearly every day brings boarders for Mr. Parker." The popularity of Parker's dock is visible below; there are several people loaded into waiting tenders for the ride to the mainland. (Courtesy of Tracy Giroux.)

SHORE VIEW, PARKERS-ON-LAKE CHAMPLAIN, NORTH HERO, VT. 44.

Ladd's Bay, now called City Bay, was the property of Jedediah Ladd, one of the earliest North Hero residents. In the early 1800s, Ladd built a landing for lake steamers dropping off passengers and shipping goods. He also erected an inn and tavern in the village facing the bay. It was a crucial community hub where town meetings, church services, and court proceedings were held. (Courtesy of Ron Fierstein.)

This bathing suit–clad family about to go for a dip in Lake Champlain demonstrates that water shoes are not only modest, but they are also protection from the rocky New England beaches. Pictured left to right in this 1910 Isle La Motte photograph are Bird Connell, Lynda Connell, Timothy Ritchie, Dorothy Connell, Betty Severance, and Annie Drugan. (Courtesy of the Isle La Motte Historical Society.)

Camp Abnaki began its life in 1901 in Charlotte, Vermont, as Camp Robinson, a YMCA summer camp for boys over age 12. Founder Byron Clark moved the camp two years later to Enfield, New Hampshire, then the following year to Chazy Lake, New York. It was not until 1906 that Clark finally held the camp at Hibbard's Point in North Hero, where it remained for a decade. (Courtesy of Ron Fierstein.)

During the 1909 camping season, the camp was permanently named Camp Abnaki in honor of the tercentenary. Enrollment rose from 21 to 75 boys, and campers began calling Clark by the nickname "Dad." Facilities at the camp were rough, boys slept in tents and a common consequence of misbehavior was a swat from Dad Clark. Note the chef made liberal use of Swift's Silver Leaf Lard. (Courtesy of Tracy Giroux.)

These 1912 campers are held up as "a study in reliable character." Indeed the camp motto, "Help the Other Fellow," typifies that sentiment. However, as a boys-only camp, clothing was occasionally viewed as optional by the summer residents. A warning system of hanging the Awasos (bear) flag upside down was devised to alert the boys to clothe themselves when women were on the grounds. (Courtesy of Tracy Giroux.)

The camp finally moved to its permanent home on Bow and Arrow Point in North Hero in 1916. Clark purchased a dance hall from the Rutland Railroad for $1, solving both his problems of the rowdy fights next door and a sorely needed kitchen/dining hall location with one fell swoop. (Courtesy of Tracy Giroux.)

Camp Abnaki had several prominent visitors over the years. Theodore Roosevelt toured the campgrounds during the 1910 season. Sir Robert Baden-Powell, founder of the Boy Scouts of America; Pres. Howard Taft; and Vice Pres. Calvin Coolidge all visited. The camp's most important person, Byron "Dad" Clark, has remained with the camp since his death in 1929; he is buried under a simple boulder on the property. (Courtesy of Tracy Giroux.)

Vacation accommodations ran the gamut of small private family cabins to large children-only campgrounds. But even in the smaller establishments, a dining room was an attractive proposition to visitors looking for a "get away from it all" experience. As standalone restaurants began opening across the islands in response to increased automobile traffic, many camps closed their dining rooms. (Courtesy of Tracy Giroux.)

The Isle La Motte baseball team was the 1934 Vermont State Champions. The team members were, from left to right, (first row) ? Jarvis and Dick LaBombard; (second row) George Lavigne and Marshall "Chappy" LaBombard; (third row) Ray Jarvis, Dan Hall, Ray Hall, Brower Hall, George Moutirele, Merritt Hall, and Harold Naylor. (Courtesy of the Isle La Motte Historical Society.)

The rise of the automobile and the relative ease of getting to and from the islands meant shorter stays for most hotel and campground guests. Instead of packing up the entire family for a summer-long adventure on the lake, visitors shifted their plans to include one- or two-week vacations with day trips sprinkled throughout the countryside in their automobiles. (Courtesy of Tracy Giroux.)

The main lodges and assembly halls of the vacation camps on Lake Champlain often featured a fireplace to take the chill off the cool Vermont nights. Card games, a shared library, comfortable seating, and even a souvenir postcard display were a common sight in these communal gathering spaces. (Courtesy of Tracy Giroux.)

These unusual homemade snowshoes are hung on display at the Hyde Log Cabin in Grand Isle. Traditional snowshoe styles usually have rawhide webbing stretched across a wooden frame of white ash; however, this heavier board style will work as well for crossing the snow. (Courtesy of the Grand Isle Historical Society.)

Pelot's Point is a long finger of North Hero directly west of the Carrying Place, which creates a long, shallow bay. It was named for Paschal Pelot, who owned 32 acres on this location in 1799. By 1806, the point marked one boundary of the first "Goal Yard," or jail, in Grand Isle County. It was later used as a campground and marina. (Courtesy of Tracy Giroux.)

South Hero's Eagle Camp (named for an eagle's nest on the site) was established on the west shore of the island in 1891 by Rev. George W. Perry and has been in continuous operation for over 117 years. Perry envisioned a "summer school of the natural sciences" open to boys and girls at alternating sessions. This 1919 photograph shows some of the 65 available tenting sites. (Courtesy of Tracy Giroux.)

KAMP KOZY, NORTH HERO, VT. 17X.

Hundreds of tiny camps sprung up across the islands as entire families spent their summers on the lake. Like Kamp Kozy in North Hero, they could be as simple as a single room with beds and a kitchenette. Others were as elaborate as miniature villages made up of tiny cottages dotting the shoreline that required a map to navigate. (Courtesy of Tracy Giroux.)

Gladys Hadd, Gerald Hadd, William Flynn, and Marion Flynn from Alburgh enjoy a picnic at Rock Point in 1941. The Flynns were active in the Alburgh community. Husband William owned a general store in town, and wife Marion was a member of the school board, first vice president of the Alburgh Library Association, and postmaster of the town. (Courtesy of the Alburgh Historical Society.)

Linger Longer, the name of this North Hero homestead, evokes the contentment and ease of spending time on the islands. The wide porch with rocking chairs and shade trees is designed for visitors to slip into a book and watch folks on the road as they go by. (Courtesy of Tracy Giroux.)

The deep profile of Lake Champlain, carved out by glaciers, means that even in the summer the water may be chilly; however, hardy Vermonters scarcely hesitate to jump in anyway. These boys may have been summer residents at Camp Abnaki or Ethan Allen Training Camp, both in North Hero. (Courtesy of Ron Fierstein.)

City Bay is located within the village of North Hero (which was occasionally known as Island City). The natural harbor created by two wooded outcroppings of land make a calm bay that is deep enough for safely anchoring a boat. City Bay was known for its crescent-shaped sandy beach and tranquil waters that beaconed swimmers. A highway reconstruction shortened the length of the beach, but the bay is still a promising fishing spot for anglers. In the winter, the iced-over lake is used for ice-fishing and Nordic skating directly across from Hero's Welcome (previously Tudhope's store). (Above, courtesy of the Vermont State Archives and Records Administration; below, courtesy of Ron Fierstein.)

CITY BAY, NORTH HERO, V.

Four

Visiting the Islands
Stores and Lodging

Ira Hill built the stone house at the Isle La Motte Corners in 1822. Throughout the end of the 19th and early 20th centuries, the building was home to the town post office, apple storage, horse stables, a tavern, a barrel shop, a restaurant, and a hotel. Hill's adjoining stone building was used as a cider mill. (Courtesy of the Isle La Motte Historical Society.)

Longtime operators of Ira Hill's boardinghouse Joseph (Josie) and Martha (Mattie) Duba purchased the hotel from the ailing Hill in 1913. The couple continued to run the establishment until the 1950s. Standing near the hotel are members of the Fleury family on Isle La Motte. (Courtesy of the Isle La Motte Historical Society.)

The brick section of John Knight's Inn at Knight's Point in North Hero was built in 1845 by John Knight Jr. He operated a ferry to Grand Isle until the first bridge opened in 1892. The wooden construction on the right is a rebuilt section of Knight Tavern, which opened in 1790. The inn is now a residence for the staff of Knight Point State Park. (Courtesy of Tracy Giroux.)

New Year's Ball

...AT...

VILLAGE HALL,

SOUTH HERO, VT.,

December 30th, 1898.

Supper at Iodine Spring House,

G. W. SQUIERS, Proprietor.

Music: North Hero Orchestra.

Hall Bill, 50c.   Supper, $1.00.

Yourself and Ladies are Cordially Invited.

FREE CARRIAGE TO AND FROM THE HALL.

The Iodine Spring House was constructed in 1868 adjacent to a mineral spring on the west shore of South Hero. The original owner, Frederick Landon, attempted to capitalize on the water's purported healing properties. After constructing a springhouse over the source and planting shade trees to cool his visitors, he then bottled and sold the water through a mail-order business. Unfortunately, Landon's plans were not profitable. After his bankruptcy, Capt. Warren Corbin took over operations at the boardinghouse. While running the inn, Corbin also supervised the construction of the steamer *Maquam* (which eventually ran between Swanton and Burlington) in Keeler's Bay from the Iodine Spring House. George W. Squiers became the third owner of the property after Corbin's wife's death in 1896. The house had rooms for up to 50 guests and a large area for special events, as seen in this 1898 dance card from a New Year's Ball. In 1925, the Iodine Spring House was destroyed by fire. (Courtesy of the South Hero Museum.)

Dec 5 - '91

W. C. Holcomb
To 68 1/2 # Corn — 75
1 Pr. Overshoe — 1.25

E. S. Fleury
24 # Nails — 1.20
1/2 # Cloves 20 Allspice 20 — 40
Oatflake 60 Coffee 120 — 1.80
Pepper 20 Dolls 30 — 50
Overshoe 50 Leggins 50 — 1.00
Rushing 20 Syrup 60 — 80

H. C. Reed
By Eggs — 1.00

Abel Phelps
Pills — 20

J. E. Bowen
5 gal Oil — 60
Sugar — 1.00

Mrs. H. Lamoreau
1 gal Oil — 15
Ink — 05
Paper — 00

Nearly 50 miles from the closest city and connected to the mainland by a single roadway, residents of Isle La Motte always worked to ensure there were enough provisions on the island. Edgar Fleury operated a general store on Main Street from 1891 until approximately 1901. Record books from December of his first year show that the Holcomb family spent $1.25 on overshoes. (Courtesy of the Turner family.)

The buildings of Birdland can still be seen directly south of the Carrying Place in North Hero. It was a summer-only luncheon restaurant with camping cabins and fishing access. The kitchen opened early for a fisherman's breakfast and is fondly remembered by patrons for its excellent soups, sandwiches, and homemade pies. (Courtesy of Tracy Giroux.)

William Naylor purchased a store from Edgar Fleury around 1906. Naylor's operated as a shop and as the post office until 1941, when he retired and Arthur Carson was appointed postmaster. Carson sold the store in 1949 and set up in a new location, just north of "the Corners," until his death in 1970. (Courtesy of the Isle La Motte Historical Society.)

The South Hero Inn began life as a tavern in 1795. This was a favored stop for farmers on their way to the market in Montreal. It was often so crowded that the only sleeping spots were on the floor. The inn, formerly known as the Island House, has changed hands many times over the centuries but continued operation as a place of lodging for nearly 200 years. (Courtesy of Ron Fierstein.)

The Sand Bar Inn was established in 1900 by Sand Bar Bridge toll collector Benajah Phelps as the Phelps House. The building (seen here in 1926) was so close to the roadway that tolls could be collected from the front porch of the house. Phelps connected a pole gate to the porch that he raised to allow drivers to pass after they had taken care of the toll. (Courtesy of Ron Fierstein.)

The Phelps House was sold and renamed the Sand Bar Inn in 1923, after Phelps had passed away. This early-1930s photograph shows the inn repainted to its original white color. In 1938, the inn was moved from the west to the east side of the tollhouse (seen on the left in both photographs) and 65 feet away from the roadside. (Courtesy of the South Hero Museum.)

The Lake-Side-Hotel, and Store, Alburgh, Vt.

After his service in the 11th Regiment Vermont Volunteers during the Civil War, Nathan Kingsley Martin spent 20 years as the customhouse inspector in the port of Alburgh, as well as a brief spell as the West Alburgh postmaster. Martin opened the Lake Side Hotel and Store in 1886 (shown here in 1921). (Courtesy of Tracy Giroux.)

The Island Villa Hotel (shown in 1921) was opened for business in the summer of 1903 by Frank and Mattie Briggs. Every guest room had spectacular lake views. Amenities included running water pumped from the lake by a windmill, electric lights powered by a generator (until 10:00 p.m.), and an icehouse available to guests for freezing fish they caught in Lake Champlain to bring home. (Courtesy of Tracy Giroux.)

Local residents joined visiting guests for Sunday dinners at the Island Villa Hotel (shown here in 1934). Pastry cook Della provided hand-cranked ice cream for lunch and dinner, and fish provided by the guests' recreational fishing was on the menu every night. Visitors also enjoyed croquet on the lawn and bridge tournaments on the wide lakeside porch. (Courtesy of Ron Fierstein.)

Tourism was, and continues to be, a major source of income for the Lake Champlain Islands. Large hotels were rare; most visitors stayed in extra bedrooms of large homes or tiny, private cottages on the lakeside. The Hazen House, near Chazy Landing, offered meals and lodging to visitors, as well as a quick route to the *Twin Boys* auto ferry. (Courtesy of the Isle La Motte Historical Society.)

In the late 1800s, the Bay Side House in East Alburgh was host to several traveling variety shows like the Mason Family Concert and Witherell's Variety Show. It was restructured 20 years later as a members-only establishment and renamed the Club House. The two buildings to the left of the Club House are the Harvey and Hayden Store and the East Alburgh Custom House. (Courtesy of the Alburgh Historical Society.)

Martell's Hotel in Grand Isle was built in 1901 to capitalize on the influx of traffic from the new Rutland Railroad. Frederick Martell built his lodging (also known as the Belmont Hotel) close to the railroad tracks, and business flourished. Martell was a man of various talents; he also worked as a rural mail carrier, blacksmith, and farmer and drove the winter stage across frozen Lake Champlain. (Courtesy of Tracy Giroux.)

Woody Nook was owned by Everett Reynolds and located near Wait's Bay on the southeast corner of Isle La Motte. John Philip Sousa was a guest here and wrote the song "Stars and Stripes Forever" while visiting the island. Woody Nook burned to the ground in 1930. (Courtesy of the Isle La Motte Historical Society.)

Vantine's, also known as the Arbor Vitae Bay House, was located in Grand Isle from the late 1800s until 1967. The lodging offered room and board for 25 guests in a main house and several cottages by the lakeside. Although Vantine's was known for fresh produce from the large garden throughout the summer, eventually it stopped serving meals because an experienced cook was difficult to find. (Courtesy of Ron Fierstein.)

Merritt Vantine also ferried passengers across the lake in the spring, summer, and fall. Locals remember heading to Vantine's for a ride to the Plattsburgh Fair. In the final days of the inn, the cabins were turned into housekeeping units; however, guests were not interested in cooking their own meals on vacation and business dwindled. The cottages and farm were sold off individually. (Courtesy of Ron Fierstein.)

BAY VIEW CABINS, NORTH HERO, VT.   D95

Without any high-rise hotels, most of the lodging on the islands is housed in large private homes or individual cabins. This affords small-scale, personal accommodations and virtually guarantees that every guest has a spectacular view of the lake. The Bay View Cabins offer rooms for two guests in each of five cottages. Today they are known as the Aqua Vista Cabins and are still hosting visitors. (Courtesy of Tracy Giroux.)

The Aqua Vista Cabins are an excellent example of Hodgson Houses, portable or prefabricated buildings invented by Ernest Franklin Hodgson in 1892. The buildings were created to be shipped in small sections that could be bolted together quickly without nails. The oldest cabin, number six, was built in the 1930s. The other cabins were added in the 1950s. (Courtesy of Tracy Giroux.)

The extraordinary explosion of color visible in the sky over the Adirondack Mountains nearly every evening explains why most of the Champlain Islands have a road named "Sunset View." In North Hero, the Sunset View cottage offers outdoor rocking chair and bench seating for the nightly event. (Courtesy of Tracy Giroux.)

The Elm Point Farm and Cottages in North Hero were operated by Paul Emile Quintin, originally from Bedford, Quebec. He opened the lakeside cabins for business in 1956. Quintin was a longtime farmer, road commissioner, and school director, as well as a member of the North Hero Volunteer Fire Department. (Courtesy of Tracy Giroux.)

Mother's Motel and Restaurant was located right on U.S. Route 2 at the North Hero Alburgh Bridge (on the North Hero side) in the 1960s. The property included two separated lodging buildings with 15 rooms, as well as a dining establishment located in a small house in front. The establishment was closed after the dining room was destroyed by fire. (Courtesy of Tracy Giroux.)

The Grand Isle Corners Store (later Minckler Brothers) was operating as early as 1831. The business changed hands at least nine times between its start and 1951. The perimeter of the store was lined with church pews where men could sit and enjoy tobacco and cigars. Residents used the store as a gathering place, especially on Saturdays when Rome Minckler raffled off chickens. (Courtesy of Ron Fierstein.)

Joseph Duba Sr. learned the blacksmith's trade in Plattsburgh before moving to Isle La Motte in 1850. His grandson George E. Duba took up the trade, and the shop (now over 125 years old) still exists with all its original contents. In January 1962, the town's historical society moved the building directly next to the south district schoolhouse. (Courtesy of the Isle La Motte Historical Society.)

In 1899, an "enterprising young merchant" named John Tudhope built a store in North Hero to compete with James Dodds's shop. Tudhope was postmaster from 1892 to 1895, and the post office was located within his store. He was also instrumental in the creation of the North Hero Community Hall in 1930. Pictured in the 1920s, the store is now home to the Hero's Welcome General Store. (Courtesy of Tracy Giroux.)

The McBride home was originally two houses, which were moved and joined in the late 1800s. This building became the Robinson Brothers store until 1915. After its closing, Juan Robinson bought up the inventory and moved it to his own establishment, the Robinson and Fifield Store. On the porch are (from left to right) Walter Irish, Charles B. Irish, William Irish, Barb ?, Charles McBride, Nellie ?. (Courtesy of the South Hero Museum.)

Robinson and Fifields Store, So. Hero Vt. 96.

Charles B. Irish established a general store at the South Hero Corners in 1885. Although maps show no building in that location, records show that he was in business until his death in 1901. After that time, the property, store, and inventory went up for sale. It passed into the hands of Amos Minckler, who sold it just six weeks later to the Keeler brothers for a $200 profit. For the next five years, the store was known as Keeler Brothers until the Keelers sold the entire operation to Juan Robinson (second from left in a vest) in 1907 for $2,250. Robinson shortly took on a partner, Orson Fifield (far right). The new store was renamed the Juan Robinson and Orson Fifield Store (seen here around 1915). Residents nicknamed it the "Concert Hall" due to the large upstairs area frequently used for community events. (Courtesy of the South Hero Museum.)

ARN'S LODGE & TAVERN -- GRAND ISLE, VERMONT   B234

The rise of automobiles meant a similar increase in the number of island visitors. These guests were no longer tied to their own boardinghouse, or even their own island, by lack of transportation. Arn's Lodge and Tavern (above) and Hazen's Lunch (below) provided welcome respite for drivers roaming the islands. These establishments offered a quick, hot meal, ice cream, and the promise of getting back on the road quickly. Some locations even provided gasoline pumps to lure drivers. Ironically, in 1904, the Vermont State Senate had attempted to stem the tide of gas- and steam-powered vehicles with a bill barring automobiles from the roadways between noon and midnight each day. The bill failed, and small businesses like these breathed a sigh of relief and saw a boom in traffic. (Above, courtesy of Ron Fierstein; below, courtesy of Tracy Giroux.)

HAZEN'S LUNCH ROOM, NO. HERO, VT.

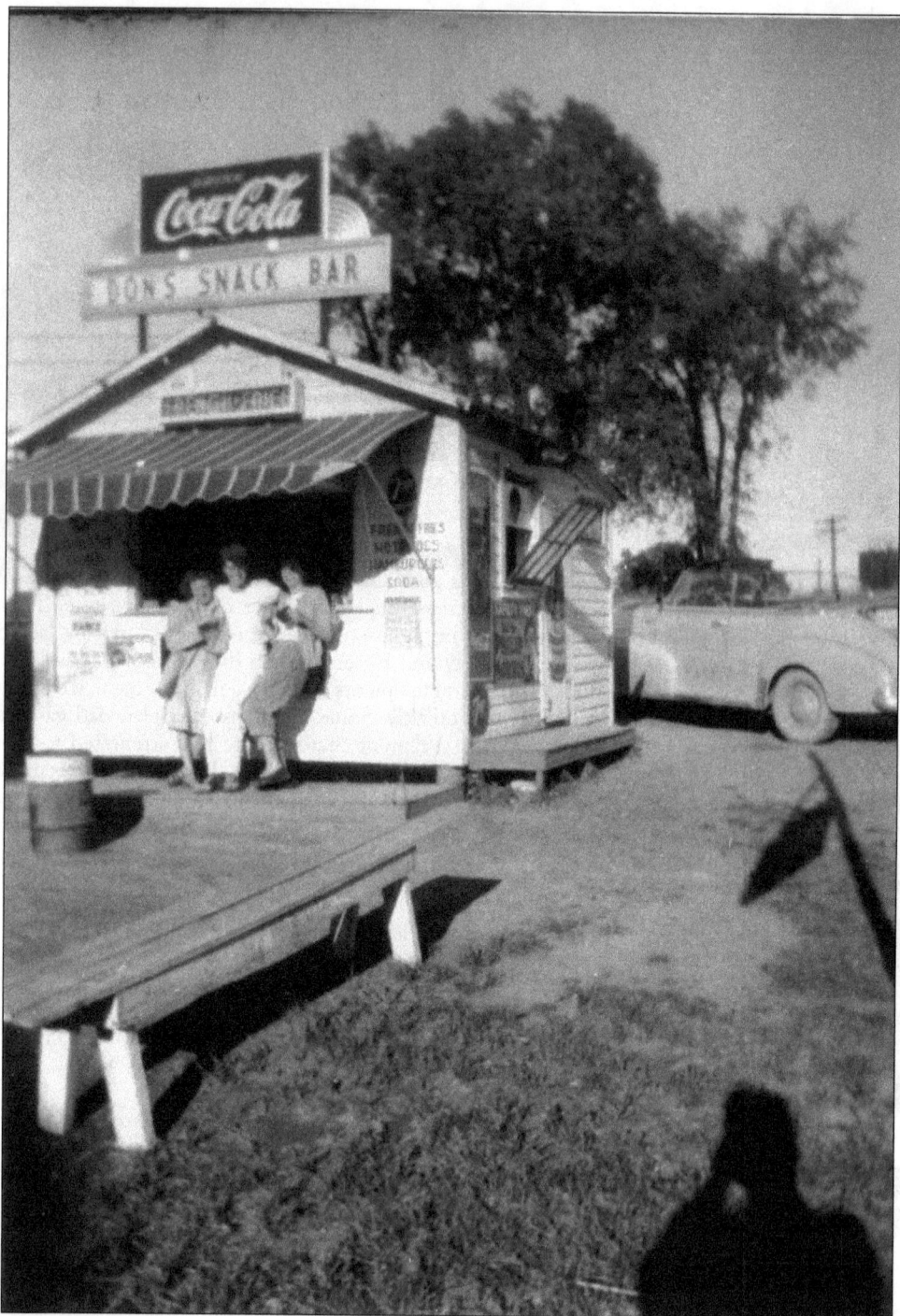

In the late 1940s, roadside sheds selling hamburgers, french fries, and sodas cropped up among the island towns. In the late 1950s, owners began serving poutine, a Canadian specialty of french fries doused in gravy and cheese curds. Don's Snack Bar, seen here in 1949 with Teresa LaBombard, Haley Ladd, and Eleanor Harnois, was located in Alburgh. (Courtesy of the Alburgh Historical Society.)

Five

INDUSTRY
QUARRIES AND WEAVING

Half a billion years ago, the Lake Champlain basin was a vast ocean filled with coral reefs. The resulting animal and mineral deposits created a major quarry industry on Isle La Motte. Although often called marble, the local rock is actually a hard limestone. It has a dark color and mottled appearance due to fossils trapped in the stone. (Courtesy of the Alburgh Historical Society.)

NELSON·W·FISK

ISLE LA MOTTE GREY AND BLACK MARBLE QUARRIES

ALL KINDS (ISLE LA MOTTE,) STREET CURBING, AND STONE
OF BUILDING AND BRIDGE VERMONT. FOR ALL STREET AND ROAD
STONE. WORK.

OUR STONE
IS LOADED ON
BOATS AT OUR QUARRY
AND SHIPPED TO NEW YORK AND
OTHER POINTS WITHOUT
RELOADING.

FISK DOCK, ISLE LA MOTTE, VT.

FISK QUARRY, ISLE LA MOTTE, VT.

POST OFFICE FISK VT._____189__

Nelson Fisk inherited Fisk Quarry from his father, Hiram, after his death in 1884. Blocks were removed from a span reaching 2,000 feet long and 30 feet high. In present years, the Fisk Quarry was purchased by the Isle La Motte Preservation Trust. Visitors can view the leftover cut quarry blocks and marvel at the fossilized coral-reef dwellers contained within the rock. (Courtesy of the Isle La Motte Historical Society.)

The island's stone resources supported five quarries throughout the town, Fisk, Fleury, Goodsell, Hill (previously known as Clark), and Wait's. Black marble from the Hill Quarry was popular in New York City for the hearths and mantels of high society. Isle La Motte marble can also be seen on the Brooklyn Bridge, the National Gallery of Art, and Radio City Music Hall. (Courtesy of the Isle La Motte Historical Society.)

Eventually Italian marble became the facade du jour and the quarries of Isle La Motte closed one by one. The Tennessee Marble Company currently sells Isle la Motte marble under the name Vermont Champlain Black. Champlain Black, or Radio Black, is the only grade A (flawless) black marble found in the United States. (Courtesy of the Vermont State Archives and Records Administration.)

Elizabeth Hubbell Fisk single-handedly brought weaving to the industrial forefront in the Champlain Islands during the arts and crafts movement. Fisk experimented with vegetable dyes and embroidery-like weaving and then later took a chemistry course at Pratt Institute to perfect her technique. She won several awards for her tapestries from organizations like the Chicago Art Institute and the Federation of Women's Clubs. (Courtesy of the Isle La Motte Historical Society.)

Elizabeth Hubbell Fisk's success in the weaving industry was initiated by her charitable works. Her first woven pieces were sold to raise money to renovate the Isle La Motte Methodist Church and to purchase a library building. Word of her exquisite work spread beyond the islands. As demand increased, local women were asked to dust off old looms and join her growing trade. (Courtesy of the Isle La Motte Historical Society.)

Fisk Looms was located in the home that Elizabeth shared with husband Nelson Fisk for 43 years. In 1923, her husband died, and her home succumbed to a devastating fire. All her materials—linen, patterns, dyes, and so on—were destroyed. She moved her business into another stone building on the property and continued work until her death in 1927. (Author's collection.)

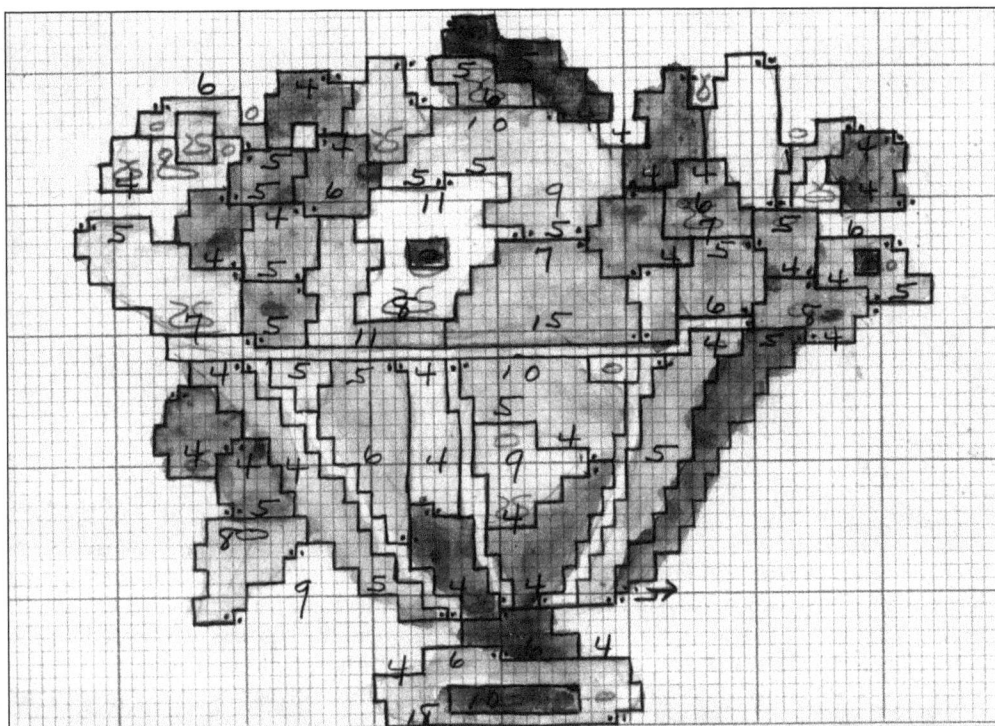

The pattern above is an original Elizabeth Fisk design. Her newly developed technique tucked loose threads back into the design itself—resulting in a finished textile that was equally as beautiful from either side. Unable to be easily mass-produced at the time, these hand-woven linen pieces were commissioned by those who appreciated the fine craftsmanship, and they are treasured by collectors today. (Courtesy of the Isle La Motte Historical Society.)

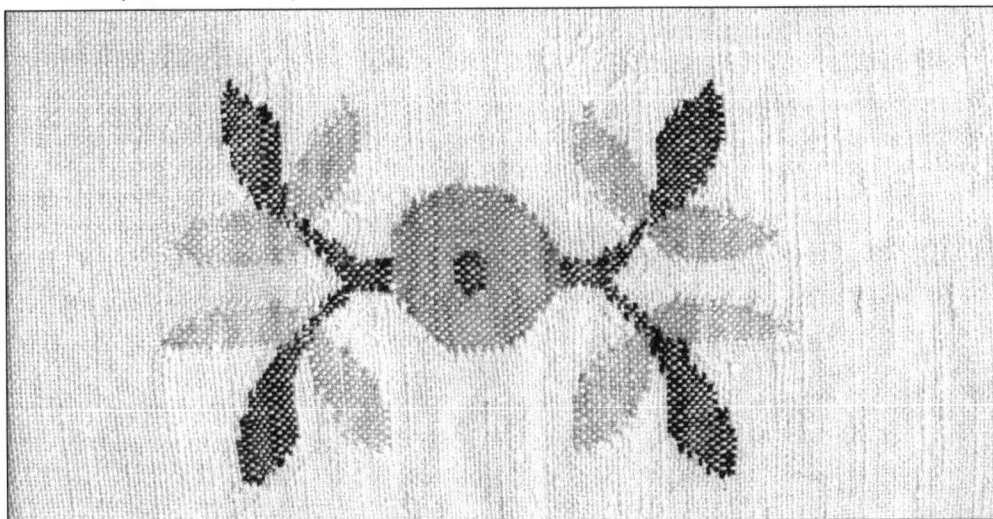

Themes drawn from nature, such as flowers, fruit, and birds, were popular motifs on Elizabeth's weavings. Her delightful pieces were frequently created for locations where they could be shown off to guests; they were primarily used as tablecloths, table runners, placemats, and framed pieces suitable for display. The apple blossom above was created for use as a dresser scarf. (Courtesy of Marty Dale.)

After the death of Elizabeth Fisk, her weaving business carried on with the women of Isle La Motte. She willed a loom to each of the women who had apprenticed with her over the years. To Cynthia Ritchie, she passed on the small stone building where the business was housed. In the photograph, Nettie Fleury is weaving in the style of Fisk. (Author's collection.)

Mabel C. Holcomb was photographed during the Craftsmen at Work Exhibition, which took place from October 28 through November 8, 1930, in the ballroom of the Hotel Styler in Boston. She gave a hands-on demonstration of Elizabeth Fisk's weaving technique and displayed finished historical textiles from Fisk Looms. (Courtesy of the Isle La Motte Historical Society.)

Six

AGRICULTURE
ORCHARDS AND DAIRY FARMS

Apples have been a cash crop for all the Lake Champlain Islands since their commercial heyday in 1890. Apples were stored in coolers locally, brought to Burlington's centralized warehouses, or hauled across the frozen lake to Plattsburgh. In the late 19th century, residents of Grand Isle lined up in wagons to use the cider press owned by Emery Paradee. (Courtesy of the Vermont State Archives and Records Administration.)

The first apple orchard planted on the islands was started around 1790 in South Hero by Col. Ebenezer Allen. Allen was a man of firsts; he is also listed as the first settler, ferry operator (between South Hero and Colchester Point), selectman, treasurer, and town clerk. The town of South Hero produced 2,341 barrels and 1,885 bushels of apples in 1877. In the same year, farmers in Grand Isle grew 2,611 barrels and 2,975 bushels of apples. In Alburgh, records as early as 1800

indicate that apples were being dried for home cooking and then pressed into cider and vinegar. Allenholm Orchards in South Hero has been operating since its 1870 start as a dairy farm. By the middle of the 20th century, apples were the primary crop at the farm. (Courtesy of the Vermont State Archives and Records Administration.)

Here a hand-cranked cider press is prepped and ready for the fall harvest. The islands' climate, slightly milder than the Vermont mainland, allowed apples to become a primary source of income for nurserymen in the 18th and 19th centuries. During one chilly fall, Wyman Holcomb's apples froze and then thawed in their barrels. The resulting juice leaked from the containers during shipping. (Author's collection.)

Apples from the islands were loaded onto ferries and ships like the *Ticonderoga* and the *Chateaugay* and brought to the mainland for use in cider and brandy. By the mid-1800s, Lake Champlain apples were well known for their quality around the globe. The *Chateaugay* (seen here) delivered pilgrims to St. Anne's Shrine in addition to picking up apple barrels. (Courtesy of the Isle La Motte Historical Society.)

Hall's Orchards in Isle La Motte has been in business since the days of Ransom Hall (1831–1911). The family orchard was passed through successive generations from Allen M. Hall to Raymond Hall and is now operated by Allen W. Hall. It remains as the last commercial apple orchard in the town. (Courtesy of the Isle La Motte Historical Society.)

Although Caleb Hill and his son Ira both operated an apple orchard on Isle La Motte, it was Ira's son Henry who took fruit production to a commercial level with new marketing and production techniques. Here barrels of Hill's apples are waiting in the fruit house for transport on steamers and railroads in 1912. (Courtesy of the Isle La Motte Historical Society.)

Apple production in the islands centered primarily on the macintosh and snow varieties; however, greenings, kings, northern spy, and spitzenberg were also cultivated locally. Capt. William Montgomery loaded his ship, the *J. T. Howard*, with 2,500 barrels of Champlain Island apples at Alburgh Springs and then posed for this 1890 photograph. (Courtesy of the Isle La Motte Historical Society.)

With the difficulties of crossing onto mainland Vermont or New York, islanders were well versed in many skills that would keep a household and farm running. Nearly every necessity was made by hand, from flaxseed and wool spun into yarn to sugar made from maple syrup. As Ira Allen commented in 1798, "The hand that guides the plow frequently constructs it." (Courtesy of the Isle La Motte Historical Society.)

Seymour and Adeline Pike proudly display their Isle La Motte–grown pumpkin. Although legend says that the town changed its name to Vineyard in 1802 because of interest in growing grapes, the petition reveals that it was the desire for a clear, easily remembered name originating in English, not agricultural leanings, prompting the change. The name reverted back to Isle La Motte in 1831. (Courtesy of the Isle La Motte Historical Society.)

Small farm stands like this 1955 booth in Grand Isle dotted the islands over the last 80 years. Many have been operated on the honor system, with owners leaving produce in the stand with a money box or coffee can and a price list tacked to the wall. According to many farmers, thefts are not common. (Courtesy of the Vermont State Archives and Records Administration.)

In 1934, the Milton Co-operative Dairy Corporation established a milk station in the town of Alburgh to service island towns with access to larger markets for their commercial dairy products. The corporation's 1935 annual report said, "This service to the remote patrons was a great convenience and a money saver. It gave them as quick service as those who lived near the main plant and saved the twenty-five cents per hundred pounds formerly paid for." In the image above, the Alburgh Creamery Yard is a hub of activity in 1945 as farmers deliver canned milk in trucks and wagons. Seen below, the creamery gets a new smokestack. (Courtesy of the Alburgh Historical Society.)

As dairy farming on the islands exploded in popularity in the early 20th century, production of dairy products like butter and cheese went from a home-based venture to a commercial affair. Farmers sold their milk to centrally located creameries that did the work of transforming the milk into other products. Cooled train cars, first with ice and then with refrigeration, made shipping possible after the opening of the Rutland Railroad Island Line. In the 1940s, the trend shifted again, and creameries began to close as distribution centers shipped raw milk directly to major cities like Boston and New York for processing. (Above, courtesy of the Vermont State Archives and Records Administration; below, courtesy of the Alburgh Historical Society.)

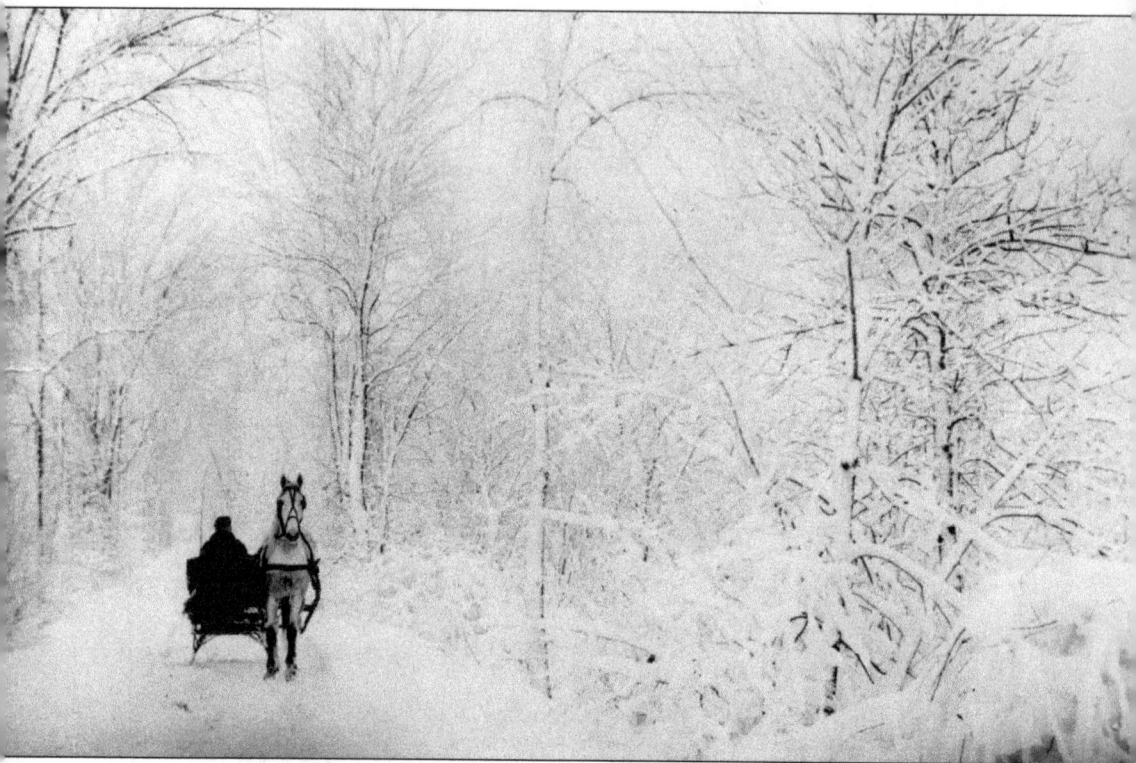

Tapping maple trees has been a hobby venture for centuries of island residents; however, with a sap to syrup ratio of 32 gallons to 1, not many local farmers had enough acreage to bring syrup-making to a commercial level. Yet even today, it is not difficult to find residents who grow a handful of sugar maples on their property for family use. A classic wintertime treat for Vermont children was sugar on snow, a simple candy made from maple syrup. The syrup was heated to the boiling point and then immediately poured onto fresh snow or shaved ice. By cooling quickly, instead of crystallizing it formed a clear and taffylike consistency that was soft and chewy. Sugar on snow (sometimes called "leather britches" because of the texture) is traditionally served with sour pickles or salted crackers to cut the sweetness of the candy. (Courtesy of the Isle La Motte Historical Society.)

Seven

CROSSING THE LAKE
SHIPS, FERRIES, AND LIGHTHOUSES

Capt. William Montgomery leans against 2,500 barrels filled with Isle La Motte apples on his schooner the *J. T. Howard*, which was docked in Alburgh Springs. Captain Montgomery's ship was one of many that brought Lake Champlain apples to international cities like London, Rio de Janeiro, and Hamburg. (Courtesy of the Isle La Motte Historical Society.)

The completion of the Champlain Canal's passage from Fort Edward, New York, to Lake Champlain in 1819 drastically increased shipping traffic around the Lake Champlain Islands. Single-masted boats called pinflats sailed with hundreds of other sailing ships in Lake Champlain in the mid- to late 19th century. Vessels including schooners, sloops, and canal boats carried passengers, produce, livestock, and lumber. Above, the *Nelson* from Montreal was captured on film around 1900, likely by budding photographer Wyman Holcomb of Isle La Motte. In the image below, a two-masted fishing schooner in winter rig (topmasts down) docks at Fisk's in Isle La Motte. (Courtesy of the Isle La Motte Historical Society.)

Souvenir Folder of
LAKE CHAMPLAIN.
STEAMER VERMONT

M

The steamer *Vermont* was put into the water in 1809. It made the five-hour journey between Fort Ticonderoga and Plattsburgh daily from May through October. With a capacity for 1,500 passengers, the *Vermont* was used in 1911 to host the New York State Historical Association's annual meeting. On October 6, the group held a lecture aboard the steamer while docked at Isle La Motte. (Courtesy of Tracy Giroux.)

The steamer *Maquam*, operated by the St. Johnsbury and Lake Champlain Railroad, docks at St. Anne's Shrine on Isle La Motte. This steamer made runs between Maquam Bay in Swanton and Burlington Harbor, often ferrying faithful pilgrims to the shrine. In the carriages are Elmer R. Houghton (right) and George Ratta (left); on shore are Cornelia and William Thomas. (Courtesy of the Isle La Motte Historical Society.)

Pilgrimages St. Anne's Shrine in Isle La Motte constituted a large part of the tourist traffic to the islands in the early 20th century. It was the height of style to take the steamer from Burlington or New York to the Champlain Islands. Pilgrims chartered steamboats like the *Chateaugay*, *Maquam*, *Reindeer*, and *Ticonderoga* (seen here); however, the World War I coal shortage brought these luxurious steamer voyages to a close. After the war, automobiles became more prevalent, and pilgrims began making the journey individually in their own cars, as thousands each year still do today. Many faithful come for morning services and then remain on the island to enjoy St. Anne's beach (open to the public) and the 13 acres of spiritual retreat on the property. Visitors can view the remains of old Fort St. Anne, which have been used to build the stations of the cross. (Courtesy of the Isle La Motte Historical Society.)

The water passage between New York State and the Lake Champlain Islands was not spanned by a bridge until 1937. The sail ferry for the Chazy, New York–Isle La Motte crossing operated from 1807 under Henry Scott and then changed hands several times until it became the domain of Franklin Hill until 1903. Hill is visible here on the ferry as it arrives around 1900. (Courtesy of the Isle La Motte Historical Society.)

In low water, Hill's sail ferry was unable to land directly adjacent to the beach. Without a dock, passengers and their goods (livestock, produce, and so on) had to wade through the water for the final few dozen feet to the shore. Occasionally rowboats were offered to make the final steps of the journey a drier proposition for ferry riders. (Courtesy of the Isle La Motte Historical Society.)

The first gas-powered ferry went into business in 1905 under the direction of William Sweet of Chazy. His original boat was named the *Twins* after Sweet's twin sons, Clinton and Gerald. It ran the route between Isle La Motte and Chazy Landing for 10 years. (Courtesy of the Isle La Motte Historical Society.)

In 1915, William sold the *Twins* and purchased a larger boat, which he called the *Twins Boys*. Sweet's ferry was able to hold 15 cars with accompanying passengers. A marvel in the islands, Sweet was host to numerous traveling dignitaries, such as Thomas Edison, Henry Ford, and Eleanor Roosevelt. Isle La Motte poet Batiste strolled the deck, passing out his poetry to passengers. (Author's collection.)

This fare schedule noted the rates for Sweet's second ferry, the *Twin Boys*, in 1920. An important clause in the ferry charter gave Sweet the right to suspend service due to unfavorable wind and weather conditions, a necessary condition given the propensity for a New England squall to arrive and leave within the space of a quarter hour. (Courtesy of the Isle La Motte Historical Society.)

Chazy Landing
AUTO FERRY
W. N. SWEET, Owner

CHAZY LANDING to ISLE LaMOTTE
NEW YORK   VERMONT

Pursuant to the authority vested in me by Chapter 71 of the Laws of 1915, I, John K. Collins, County Judge of Clinton County, New York, do hereby order, direct and determine the following rates and conditions of ferriage for the Chazy Landing Automobile Ferry.

SCHEDULE OF RATES
(Automobiles and Motor Vehicles)

1st. Automobile, one way, $1.25 for car and driver. 25c. for each passenger.

2nd. Trip tickets issued in books of six on sale at the ferry. Price of the books, $7.50. Good until used. Each ticket good for passage one way for automobile, driver and passenger.

3rd. Motorcycles, 75c. for machine and driver. 25c. for each extra passenger.

TEAMS. Teams, single or double, 75c.

FOOT PASSENGERS, 25c. each, one way. If special trip is made, no charge less than 75c.

HORSES, CATTLE, SHEEP, CALVES AND SWINE, 25c. a head, one way.

HOURS OF OPERATION. A boat, or boats, shall be kept in readiness and operated between the hours of daylight and dark, with the privilege of operating the ferry before daylight and after dark, if the owner, William N. Sweet, so desires. The owner, William N. Sweet, may refuse to operate the ferry at any and all times when wind and weather create conditions which, in the judgment of the said owner, are unsafe, and may refuse to transport motor trucks of such weight and dimensions as, in the judgment of said owner, are unsafe.

(Signed,) JOHN K. COLLINS,

Dated, the 1st day of May, 1920.   Clinton County Judge.

Connecting the direct route between Burlington, Montreal, Plattsburgh, Adirondacks, and Trunk Line between Maine, Potsdam, Ogdensburg and all points west.

New Boat. Capacity, 15 Touring Cars. Sterling Engines, 110 H. P.

One-way rates were $1.25 for a vehicle and passenger, plus 25¢ for each additional person. Interestingly, fares for horses, cattle, sheep, and swine were equal to that of a human passenger. Sweet's ferry operated from dawn until sunset until 1936, when the Alburgh-Rouses Point Bridge was built and travelers no longer needed to cross by boat. (Author's collection.)

Horace Corbin began ferry service between Grand Isle and Cumberland Head in 1917 with a boat called the *Keeler Bay*. After one year, he replaced the ferry with another that was easier to maneuver called the *Kittery*. Corbin, seeking a bigger boat, sold the *Kittery* after just two years of service and bought the 144-foot *Roosevelt*. He eventually purchased the Lake Champlain Transportation Company in 1937 and ran the *Ticonderoga*, *Vermont*, and *Chateaugay* steamers. The *Roosevelt* ferry ran for 36 years before leaks in the hull forced the company to intentionally sink her in the lake in 1959. (Courtesy of Ron Fierstein.)

The 220-foot steamer *Ticonderoga* was built in 1906 and based out of Burlington. The side-wheel steamer (a day boat and ferry) stopped at ports along the New York and Vermont sides of Lake Champlain from April until December. The ship was retired in 1953 and was painstakingly preserved. It is open to the public as a hands-on exhibit at the Shelburne Museum in Vermont. (Courtesy of Tracy Giroux.)

During the days of Lake Champlain's use as a main travel route between New York, Vermont, and Canada, houseboats (offering housing and transportation in one) were a common sight along the shoreline. Often, houseboat residents jockeyed for the best position along the docks. In some cases, they sabotaged each others' positions by cutting tether lines and setting boats adrift during the night. (Courtesy of the Isle La Motte Historical Society.)

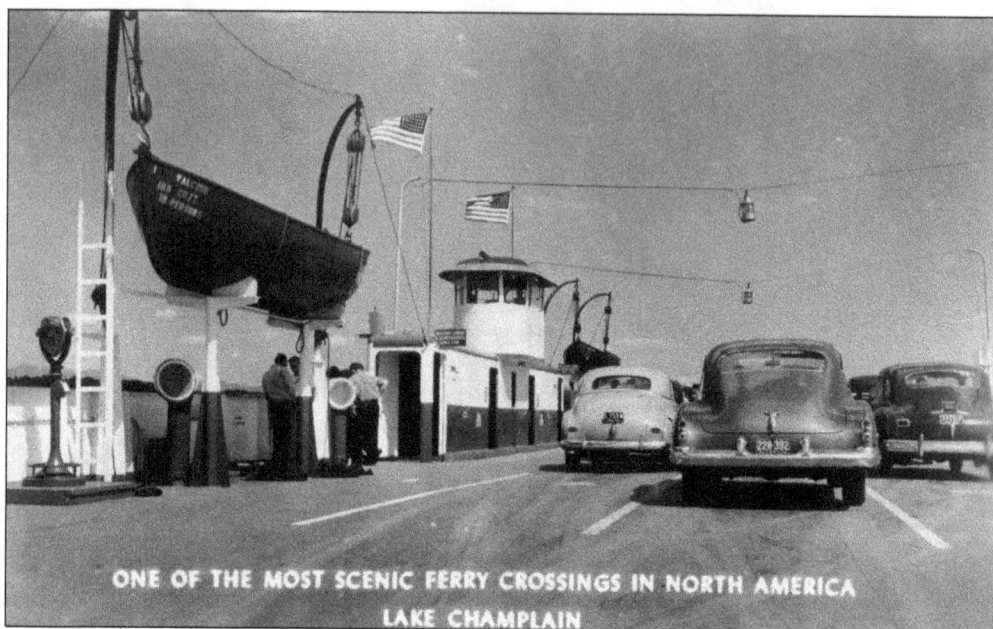

ONE OF THE MOST SCENIC FERRY CROSSINGS IN NORTH AMERICA
LAKE CHAMPLAIN

The Lake Champlain Ferry Company purchased the *Valcour* ferryboat in 1947 to make the trip between Burlington and Port Kent. Filled to capacity, it could hold 50 cars and offered passengers a lounge and restrooms for the journey. It still runs the hour-long route today during the spring, summer, and fall. (Courtesy of Ron Fierstein.)

The first lighthouse on Isle La Motte was actually only a lantern set into a second-floor window of Ezra Pike Jr.'s home in 1829. It was not until 30 years later that a dedicated structure was built as a beacon; a stone pyramid holding a lantern was tended by a farmer who often allowed the light to go out during stormy weather. (Courtesy of the Isle La Motte Historical Society.)

Wilbur F. Hill was the keeper of the Isle La Motte lighthouse for nearly 50 years from 1871 until 1919. During his tenure, Hill received several awards for keeping the most reliable lighthouse station in the district. In this 1919 photograph, he poses in his duty uniform. (Courtesy of the Isle La Motte Historical Society.)

In 1879, the U.S. government commissioned a cast-iron lighthouse and keeper's house. Over the years, the lighthouse's original orange paint has faded to a distinct salmon pink, often called "Nantucket Red." The 25-foot-high lighthouse was replaced by a skeleton tower four years after keeper Hill's death in 1919; however, the beacon was returned to active service in 2002. (Courtesy of the Isle La Motte Historical Society.)

It is hard to imagine today, looking at the calm waters and occasional pleasure craft skimming by, but Lake Champlain was once a highway on water. With no railroad in the area until the late 1800s and a road system made piecemeal by a lack of permanent bridges, boats were the only reliable means of transportation between the islands and the rest of the world. Over the course of the area's commercial prime, there were thousands of over 60 different types of ship afloat at any given time. As seen in this Elizabeth Fisk weaving, ships were part and parcel of life on the lake. Rafts, ferries, pinflats, canal boats, schooners, and steamers all shared the waterways, leading to some inevitable disasters. Below the surface of the lake, over 60 shipwrecks from the 18th, 19th, and 20th centuries often lie where divers can view their remains. (Courtesy of the Isle La Motte Historical Society.)

Eight

ON THE GROUND
BRIDGES AND RAILROADS

The bridge between South Hero and Milton was originally a natural sandbar that appeared when the lake level was low, but the crossing could only be completed with a combination of riding and swimming. In 1850, a new bridge was completed using slate pieces from the lakeshore. The single-lane road was wide enough for one wagon, so turnouts were built for safe passing. (Courtesy of Ron Fierstein.)

The rebuilt Sand Bar Bridge was a relief to islanders, who finally had a reliable passage to the mainland; however, as fast as the Sand-Bar Bridge Company made repairs, the elements battered the structure. In the spring, the bridge was often covered by large chunks of migrating ice, which pushed boulders onto the roadway where they remained after the ice had melted (photograph above). At the same time, warm-weather thaws could sufficiently raise the level of the lake to submerge the road surface completely (photograph below). The company never made profits or paid dividends to shareholders. (Above, courtesy of the Vermont State Archives and Records Administration; below, courtesy of Ann Wetzel.)

The Sand Bar Bridge was reconstructed again in 1922 with a five-year project budget of $75,000. The roadway was flanked by large quarry rocks instead of a guardrail, and it was reported that local drivers frequently had to "take to the rocks" to avoid overly cautious tourists who drove in the center of the roadway to avoid the rocks. (Courtesy of Ron Fierstein.)

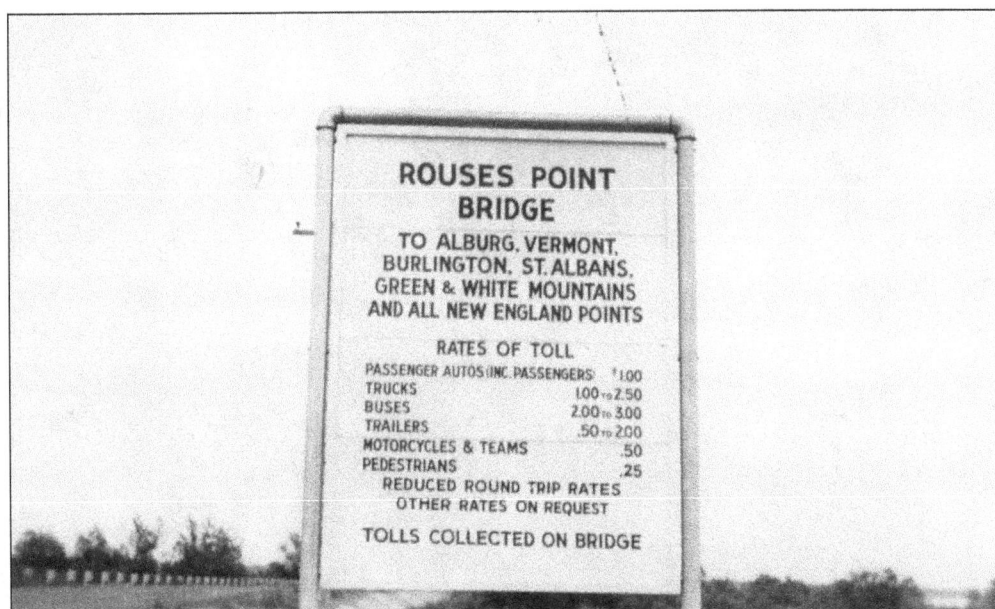

Making the Alburgh to Rouses Point, New York, crossing was done by ferry until 1938 when the Rouses Point Bridge was built to complete the highway between Swanton, Vermont, and New York State. With several bridges requiring hefty tolls, traveling through the islands was not an inexpensive affair; however, it was greatly preferred to the unpredictable ferry crossings used in the past. (Courtesy of the Vermont State Archives and Records Administration.)

The only span connecting the Champlain Islands was the Sand Bar Bridge between South Hero and mainland Vermont, until 1882, when Isle La Motte bridged the gap to Alburgh. All other travel between the islands had to be made by boat. In 1892, the citizens of Grand Isle voted to create their own crossing between Grand Isle and North Hero. They constructed a swing bridge,

which pivots 90 degrees horizontally from a center point to allow boat traffic to pass. The motion of the bridge was controlled by the tender's hand crank. On blustery days, fishermen (or the tender's wife) had to be called upon to help open the span against the wind. (Courtesy of the Vermont State Archives and Records Administration.)

In the late 19th century, crossing the lake between Alburgh and North Hero had to be completed on John O'Neill's ferry. Rough waves and high winds could often call off a trip. In 1884, representatives from North Hero petitioned the Vermont General Assembly for $25,000 to build a permanent bridge across the span. Residents shrewdly invited the committee members to make the crossing by boat in the fall, just as the locals had to do. Not surprisingly, the committee voted to give the town the full amount of its proposal after their hair-raising ride across the channel. The new iron bridge was completed on October 28, 1886. It featured a double-draw span that could be cranked open (by hand) to allow boats to pass. The bridge was rebuilt in 1954 and is still in use today. (Courtesy of Tracy Giroux.)

In 1887, islanders soon realized that bridge tender Spellman Hazen lived far enough away from the North Hero-Alburgh Bridge that he did not always see teams riding across. This meant a toll-free crossing for anyone lucky enough to escape his watch. Sixty years later, Henry Martin balances on the top of the bridge's iron girders shortly before its 1954 demolition and reconstruction. (Courtesy of Robin Gutierrez.)

A work crew completes the railroad trestle between East Alburgh and the Vermont mainland at Swanton. An attempt to build an automobile bridge between the two towns failed in 1928 because of the Great Depression. Work restarted in June 1936 but faltered again when the builders burned through their funds. The Vermont State Highway Board finished the project, and the new bridge opened in 1938. (Courtesy of Robin Gutierrez.)

Myron B. Holcomb was officially employed as the Isle La Motte-Alburgh Bridge tender, and he was charged with maintaining the safety of all vessels and people crossing the span. The fare for automobiles was 25¢ one way and 30¢ round-trip—"strangers" paid a higher rate of 30¢. At the time, the town derived substantial income via tolls collected from those entering the area from Alburgh, which served to keep resident taxes low. This crossing remained a toll bridge until 1944, long after all other crossings into the islands had become free. On June 15, 1936, at 9:45 p.m., Holcomb shot and killed a 26-pound lynx from Canada on the bridge. (Courtesy of the Isle La Motte Historical Society.)

In 1953, after 60 years of service, the State of Vermont replaced the old hand-cranked Grand Isle-North Hero swing bridge with an electric drawbridge. In this aerial photograph, taken after the new bridge was dedicated, Knight Point State Park is visible in the foreground and Grand Isle's Ladd Point is in the background. (Courtesy of the Vermont State Archives and Records Administration.)

During the rebuilding of U.S. Route 2 in Alburgh during June 1970, this bulldozer and pan scraper were used to grade the roadbed before resurfacing. The historic dirt and gravel roads throughout the islands require continuous special care to avoid potholes and washouts. Snowy winters, freeze-thaw cycles, and high waves washing over the roads create a need to regrade the surfaces. (Courtesy of the Vermont State Archives and Records Administration.)

Started in 1899, the Rutland Railroad offered a route that started from Burlington, passed through the Champlain Islands, and continued on to Rouses Point, New York. Several water crossings made the railroad a pricey proposition, and although it had several decades of service bringing milk and passengers to and from the area, it struggled in later years and finally had its last run on September 25, 1961. (Courtesy of Tracy Giroux.)

The Isle La Motte railroad station, which was actually located on the southern end of the Alburgh peninsula, allowed the creation of the first passenger train route between Alburgh and Burlington in 1899. The Island Line operated with six passenger trains (plus two extra in the summer months) and two milk trains for over 60 years. (Courtesy of the Isle La Motte Historical Society.)

The Alburgh railroad station was a stop along the Rutland-Canadian Railroad, which later became the Island Line. The Green Mountain Flyer brought not only passengers and commodities, but jobs for locals such as unloading cars, controlling weeds between ties, providing ice for dairy trains carrying butter and milk, and leveling track that had shifted with winter frost heaves. (Courtesy of the Alburgh Historical Society.)

Lecturers and railroad officials gathered at the South Hero train station for the July 1910 Better Farming Special Train. The train was a traveling exhibition of agricultural information offered by the Agricultural Extension Service. Attendees attended lectures, viewed exhibits, participated in demonstrations, and were encouraged to ask questions pertaining to livestock and crops. (Courtesy of the Vermont State Archives and Records Administration.)

Alburgh station was on the Ogdensburg and Lake Champlain route, bringing dairy products from northern towns to Boston and New York City. These Alburgh men are constructing a water tower in the rail yard. A milk car destined for the Whiting Milk Company in Boston was filled and picked up in Alburgh. Other stations along the line added cars containing cream and ice-cream mix. (Courtesy of Robin Gutierrez.)

A Fine View of the Round House and Yard, Alburgh, Vt.

Some 18 minutes away from the South Alburgh station, the actual Alburgh station was the last stop in Vermont before the Island Line crossed into New York at Rouses Point and then headed north into Canada toward Montreal. In 1905, Alburgh boasted a full rail yard with turntable and roundhouse, as well as a tiny housing development (seen behind the water towers) called Sabreville. (Courtesy of the Alburgh Historical Society.)

The freezing over of Lake Champlain created jobs for the men of Alburgh. Ice harvesting for the Rutland Railroad Island Line (here in the 1930s) took place in Windmill Bay. The frozen blocks were brought to a local icehouse and stored for cooling dairy and produce cars. The annual harvest lasted until 1935, when the advent of refrigerator cars made ice blocks obsolete. (Courtesy of the Alburgh Historical Society.)

With finances floundering, the Rutland Railroad reorganized into the Rutland Railway in 1950. Two years after this August 1948 photograph, the two Rutland-Alburgh local trains ceased operations. The sight of people on the platform became a rarity after 1953, when the railroad stopped offering passenger service altogether. (Courtesy of the Alburgh Historical Society.)

The Rutland Railroad was originally leased to the Vermont Central Railroad for 119 years; however, when its parent company went bankrupt in 1896, the railroad became independent once again. On the Vermont lines, flangers were used to clear snow and ice from the tracks. Because the blades hung below track level, signs alerted operators to raise their blades to clear crossings and other obstacles. (Courtesy of the Alburgh Historical Society.)

Nine

NOTABLE NAMES
PROMINENT PEOPLE, LOCATIONS,
AND CELEBRATIONS

The Hyde Log Cabin in Grand Isle (original location shown), constructed by Jedediah Hyde in 1783, is known as one of the oldest remaining log cabins in the United States. Hyde was a surveyor in Lamoille County, Vermont, and wintered as a schoolteacher in Massachusetts and Pawlet, Vermont. He did not live full time on the Grand Isle (then called Middle Hero) until 1790. (Courtesy of the Grand Isle Historical Society.)

The cabin stood untouched until 1945, when the owner, Coleman Cota, decided to disassemble the logs for lumber. Interested residents held a fund-raising drive and collected enough money to move the cabin adjacent to Route 2. With much fanfare, the Hyde Log Cabin was moved two miles southwest in 1946. Local children were given the day off from school to watch the event. (Courtesy of the Vermont State Archives and Records Administration.)

Restoration of the one-room home took place sporadically over the next 40 years as funds became available. The one-room structure was given a working reproduction fireplace in 1949 (seen here with artifacts from the period) and a new roof in 1985. The cabin stands as a museum today. (Author's collection.)

Another venerable log cabin on the islands belonged to the Rochester family in Isle La Motte. Built after 1865, when John Rochester moved to the island from England, it housed his daughter, Elda Ann Rochester, for 64 years. After her death in 1925, Harold Hayden bought the cabin and moved it to his property on the northern point of the island. (Courtesy of the Isle La Motte Historical Society.)

In July 1794, the Grand Isle County militia surrounded the British blockhouse on Block House Point after an alert that skirmishes could break out at any moment. The British troops held their ground tactfully and did not engage the American soldiers, but they also did not give up the spot until 1796. Block House Point would become the eventual location of the Ethan Allen Training Camp. (Courtesy of Tracy Giroux.)

Cloak Island, off the eastern shore of Isle La Motte, gets its name from a domestic quarrel in the 1770s. Eleanor Fisk, fed up with her husband's angry tirades, hitched up her team and headed across frozen Lake Champlain for the mainland. She never returned, but her red cloak was found on the small island. She was presumed drowned, and Fisk remarried. (Courtesy of the Isle La Motte Historical Society.)

The Hyde Log Cabin collection features this 1886 photograph of Jennie and Florence Watkins, ages seven and five respectively. These girls were the children of Charles and Juliana (Jackson) Watkins. Juliana was the granddaughter of the cabin's original owner, Jedediah Hyde Jr. The Watkins family moved to Massachusetts in 1880; it is likely that this photograph was sent back to relatives in Grand Isle. (Courtesy of the Grand Isle Historical Society.)

KEELERS BAY FROM SQUIRES LOOKOUT, So. HERO, VT. 94A.

Keeler's Bay in South Hero is named for Abner Keeler (1778–1852), who lived and worked as a farmer and merchant in that area of the town. Keeler was very successful at his trade; he owned a retail establishment and several farms. Justice of the peace records from the town tell the story of Edward Reoux, who tapped a barrel of Keeler's alcohol but closed it so poorly that 50 gallons of the St. Croix spirits (likely rum) leaked from the tap and was unusable. Keeler sued for the $80 loss and after two trials, he was awarded $25 in damages. Unfortunately for Keeler, Reoux had nothing to his name except for one cow worth $8, and he was never able to recover the value of his lost liquor. (Courtesy of Ron Fierstein.)

KEELERS BAY, SOUTH HERO, VT. 29.

The Irving House was built in 1896 by James H. and Nellie Newton Dodds. It boasted the first bathroom in North Hero and a modern central heating system, welcome luxuries for weary travelers. Steamers arrived two to three times daily, carrying guests from neighboring cities and states. In 1902, records show that Dodds was able to host 20 guests at a rate of $2 per day (board included). (Courtesy of Tracy Giroux.)

Dodds generously offered a free shuttle from the railroad for all incoming guests. He also permitted the use of his facilities by the citizens of North Hero for dances and other social occasions during the winter when business was slow. Irving House was passed on to Dodds's son Donald in 1944 and then sold in 1970. Today the four buildings are operated as the North Hero House. (Courtesy of Tracy Giroux.)

The Grand Isle County Courthouse was built in 1824. The walls of the courthouse were constructed with Isle La Motte limestone cut two and a half feet thick. The building included a dining room, a poor-debtors room, and a jail. The courthouse was remodeled in 1903; one of the principal improvements was the addition of indoor toilets. Just over 100 years later, the bell tower was restored as well. (Courtesy of Tracy Giroux.)

The stone house on the south end of Isle La Motte was built in 1828 for Elihu Hall and housed services for the Methodist Church for a number of years. Hall was a selectman for 11 terms from 1794 until 1835 and tended a thriving apple orchard. The home has been in the family for 180 years and now houses a cafe. (Courtesy of the Isle La Motte Historical Society.)

This tintype of Caleb P. Hill was taken in the mid-1820s and was carefully framed with a matching image of his wife, Mercy Pike. The Hill family operated a ferry between Alburgh and Isle La Motte (called Vineyard at the time) from 1805 until August 14, 1882, when a bridge crossing the span was opened for travelers. (Courtesy of the Isle La Motte Historical Society.)

As a young man, Seneca Harold Pike was witness to a tragic series of events in Isle La Motte history. In 1843, a peddler named Pipershine came to town and found lodging with Pike family. Early one morning, while Pike's mother, Barbara, was doing chores, the peddler inexplicably stabbed her several times. She lived for a month and then died from her wounds. (Courtesy of Betty and Robert Pike.)

Nelson Fisk was a prominent Vermonter who resided in Isle La Motte. He was elected lieutenant governor in 1896 and became a friend to a handful of U.S. presidents, like William McKinley and Theodore Roosevelt. Fisk set up a post office in his general store (of which he was postmaster) known as Fisk, Vermont. His method of mixing store and stamp purchases caused great consternation among postal inspectors. Fisk countered their annoyance by pulling a $100 bill from a drawer and saying, "This office is permitted $100 worth of stamp stock. Here is a $100 bill. Any time you want it, this belongs to the post office, and all the stamps belong to me!" He was also known for his well-timed business decisions. During one mild winter, the Hudson River failed to freeze and residents of New York City found themselves without ice. Fisk brought his Lake Champlain ice down to the city and made a small fortune that allowed him to completely renovate his home. (Courtesy of the Isle La Motte Historical Society.)

Lt. Gov. Nelson Fisk's home was the location for many noted Champlain Islands events. Pres. William McKinley visited in 1897, and Vice Pres. Theodore Roosevelt came for an ill-fated visit in 1901. It was here that wife Elizabeth Fisk began her weaving business. At various times the property hosted a store, post office, and several grand banquets. The mansion was burned to the ground in 1923. (Courtesy of the Isle La Motte Historical Society.)

The border between Vermont and Canada has not always been a peaceful one. In 1792, nearly a decade after hostilities ended, British soldiers from Quebec surrounded and captured prominent Alburgh men (a constable, deputy sheriff, and magistrate) during several separate incidents along the border. These actions, and the ensuing correspondence between Gov. Thomas Chittenden and the governor of Quebec, nearly reignited the Revolutionary War. (Courtesy of the Alburgh Historical Society.)

In September 1901, Vice President Roosevelt dined on Isle La Motte during an address to the Vermont Fish and Game League. The event was held at Fisk Farm and drew hundreds of people from around the state. After a brief welcome reception on the porch, guests gathered in the immense tent set up on the lawn. (Courtesy of the Isle La Motte Historical Society.)

At 5:30 p.m., a telephone call came in to the Fisk home with news that President McKinley had been shot at the Pan-American Exposition in Buffalo. Roosevelt immediately left the shocked attendees and boarded a special train headed for the exposition. McKinley died of shock and gangrene eight days later, and Roosevelt assumed the presidency. (Courtesy of the Isle La Motte Historical Society.)

Locals celebrate the more festive portions of Theodore Roosevelt's visit to the islands with a commemorative Teddy Roosevelt Day held annually in September. The gathering features apple-themed events, volunteers in period costume, and a guest appearance by Roosevelt. At Fisk Farm (seen above in 1901 before the fateful call) visitors sip tea in the same location where Roosevelt heard the devastating news. (Courtesy of the Isle La Motte Historical Society.)

This early-1890s photograph was taken at the Waterbury House in South Hero, and seen are, from left to right, Mary Clark Landon Wheeler holding daughter Frances Wheeler, Rev. Orville Wheeler, Henry Wheeler, Sheldon Wheeler, and Frances Mary Wheeler. Reverend Wheeler was called to be pastor of the South Hero-Grand Isle Congregational Church in 1840. (Courtesy of the South Hero Museum.)

George H. Perkins, Ph. D., state geologist and professor of geology at the University of Vermont, visited the Champlain Islands in 1902 to examine shale specimens along the shoreline. Perkins was excited to find many fine specimens of shale for study. He wrote of this particular cliff, "It is difficult to imagine a more complete example of superlative folding and crushing than this cliff affords." (Courtesy of Ron Fierstein.)

The following announcement about the proposed building of Lockwood Hall on Main Street in Alburgh (here in 1910) appeared in the St. Albans *Weekly Messenger* on January 19, 1905, "H. C. Jameson has sold the foundation formerly occupied by the store of the late Nelson Young, to N. R. Lockwood who will erect a building soon." (Courtesy of the Alburgh Historical Society.)

On the southern tip of Isle La Motte, Peter Fleury (1813–1878) owned a brick house as well as 220 acres, which included his quarry. After Fleury's death, his widow Christiana and sons Edgar and Harry inherited the home. Edgar became a prominent townsperson, acting as constable, deputy sheriff, postmaster, Grand Isle County representative, and assistant judge in the Grand Isle County Court. (Courtesy of the Turner family.)

In the mid-1950s, Peter Fleury's grandson (also named Peter) sold his property, encompassing much of the southern tip of Isle La Motte, to Selby Turner. In the summer of 1961, the Turner family moved the brick house from its original location to a spot near the lakeside. Some 20 years later, the family also moved the Fleury barn and converted it into a summer residence. (Courtesy of the Turner family.)

In 1909, 300 years after the first European settlement, Vermont, New York, and Quebec jointly celebrated their tercentennial anniversary. Prominent island residents and visiting dignitaries gathered at St. Anne's Shrine to kick off the events. In attendance (fourth from the left) was Charles Evans Hughes, then governor of New York, later to become chief justice of the United States Supreme Court. (Courtesy of the Isle La Motte Historical Society.)

Hon. Henry Hill of Isle La Motte was a key organizer of the tercentenary. He presented the original resolution to the New York State Senate (of which he was a member in 1907) requesting a celebration to honor Samuel de Champlain's arrival. The resolution was adopted on April 15, 1907, and a commission was created to coordinate the event. (Courtesy of the Isle La Motte Historical Society.)

The statewide tercentenary celebration brought thousands of visitors to the Lake Champlain Islands. One of the main attractions was an expansive pageant of Native Americans, presented by 168 descendants of the Iroquois just off the shores of Isle La Motte. In the same waters, the participants reenacted the battle of Lake Champlain and presented a dramatic interpretation of Henry Wadsworth Longfellow's *Hiawatha*. (Courtesy of the Isle La Motte Historical Society.)

Although extensive, the Native American pageants were also portable; during the proceedings, they were moved on a 300-foot float to various locations on the lake. Additional local events during the seven-day celebration included military and naval exercises, speeches, the dedication of several monuments and plaques in all three locations, and a visit from Pres. Theodore Roosevelt. (Courtesy of the Isle La Motte Historical Society.)

The Lady Chapel at Westerly was born when Maria Moulton Graves hired the services of a famous Chicago church architect to design the tiny chapel for her family's use on their Grand Isle property. Graves adored the property and diminutive chapel. In a 1914 poem, she wrote of it, "The Chapel speaks. It tells of those we love; Pure hearts and true, with us but yester-year." (Courtesy of Ron Fierstein.)

One of the first structures erected on the Westerly property was the pavilion that Graves built. It was used as an everyday recreation spot, as well as decorated with lanterns for special events like birthdays. During any given summer, the family plus visiting friends could equal nearly 100 guests. (Courtesy of Ron Fierstein.)

Helena Holcomb Skeels was the first female representative from Grand Isle County. Of this photograph, she said, "That picture was taken in 1910. I was the first woman in Grand Isle County to have a car. It was a scarlet Maxwell, weighed 1,400 lbs - had two shifts forward and one backwards." (Courtesy of the Isle La Motte Historical Society.)

The Carrying Place, as named by the Abenaki Indians in the area, is a narrow piece of land connecting two sections of North Hero Island. In this spot, natives and settlers alike had quick access to mainland Vermont from the west side of North Hero over a portage of three to four rods (15–20 feet). This area was also a favorite shortcut for smugglers. (Courtesy of Ron Fierstein.)

In 1910, going south down the center of Main Street in Alburgh, visitors would find the William E. Flynn General Store and post office, a customhouse, and Ora Bell's hotel called the Bell House. The hotel and customhouse were destroyed by fire in 1918, but the general store building is still in use today. During the 1930s, the U. S. Post Office changed the name of the town to Alburg, dropping the final h despite the protests of the town. In 2006, residents officially voted to return the name to its original state. (Courtesy of the Alburgh Historical Society.)

Juan Robinson stands in front of the home he shared with wife Sarah Gordon in South Hero. Robsinson was a prominent man who lived in the town for all his life. He began working as a farmer and became a state senator, a selectman, and a director of the Sand Bar Bridge Company. Robinson was best known as the 25-year proprietor of the Robinson and Fifield Store. (Courtesy of Ron Fierstein.)

Susan McBride of South Hero, second from right, waited tables at Mother's Lunch in 1951. Susan tells the tale of a strange-looking man who ordered his steak raw one afternoon. She brought back a rare steak, but the customer demanded raw meat. The owner, Mr. Sims, explained that they could not serve raw meat, and the customer left in a huff. (Courtesy of Susan McBride Crowley.)

Paved roads, automobiles, and scattered gasoline filling stations (a Texaco logo is visible on the right-hand side) reveal the town's infrastructure improvements in this 1941 photograph of Alburgh's town center. By this time, the population in the town had reached a 20th-century high of 1,623; however, the Rutland Railroad Island Line, which brought jobs and tourists to the area, was feeling a financial pinch. (Courtesy of the Alburgh Historical Society.)

In 1959, Champlain Islanders celebrated the 350th anniversary of the discovery of Lake Champlain by Samuel de Champlain with a fleet of boys in a "canoecade" wearing French explorer and Native American costumes. This landing is also reenacted annually by a flotilla of vessels (both hand- and engine-powered) circling the shores of Isle La Motte. (Courtesy of the Vermont State Archives and Records Administration.)

Isle La Motte poet D. T. (Dan) Trombley (1849–1940) published under the name Batiste for 20 years, including the book *Batiste of Isle La Motte and His Trubbles* in 1915. Batiste's writing career began when he was nearly 60 years old. Before that time, he worked on the railroad, farmed, and was proprietor of the Lake View Cottage boardinghouse. (Courtesy of the Isle La Motte Historical Society.)

THE OLD STONE CHURCH

Isle La Motte, Vermont

I have in mind an old stone church, to me so very dear;
Which I've attended off and on for more than three score year.
Through cold spring rain and summer heat, and winter's ice and snow,
Between my home and this old church, I've travelled to and fro.

When first I sat within the pews of this old church of stone,
I was surrounded by dear friends that I could call my own.
The ones who filled the pews those days now sleep beneath the sod;
But three are left besides myself; The others are with God.

And as I pause and look around, no others do I see;
Of them who filled the pews those days, there's no one left but me.
And younger ones now take the place of those gone on ahead;
A few years more and they, too, will be numbered with the dead.

Batiste composed this poem for Old Home Day in 1938. He was known to frequent William Sweet's Isle La Motte–Chazy ferry, distributing copies of his writing. Local lore has it that he once wrote a song about "Ma" Fisk's eventual return to life, which so nettled Nelson Fisk that he gave another man a cow to persuade him to stop singing Batiste's jingle. (Courtesy of the Isle La Motte Historical Society.)

The islands' climate is generally milder than either the New York or Vermont mainland on either side, and winter snowfall is typically not overwhelming. But strong winds racing between the Adirondack Mountains to the west and the Green Mountains to the east buffet the islands and can cause blinding whiteout conditions when snow is on the ground. A driver navigates a single-lane road after a storm. (Courtesy of Ron Fierstein.)

Rarely a blizzard dumps several feet of snow on the islands and lake. Narrow gravel roads with no shoulders make snow removal a tedious process, and few redundancies in the power grid in the area make multiple days without electricity following a storm a very real possibility. The Hadd children enjoy playing atop a high winter snowbank behind their house in Alburgh. (Courtesy of the Alburgh Historical Society.)

Hen Island is one of roughly 80 small islands in Lake Champlain, and it is located just off the City Bay shoreline in North Hero. Measuring less than a quarter acre, the grassy shale outcroppings on the island are a nesting place for endangered terns. It is now managed by the Nature Conservancy. (Courtesy of Ron Fierstein.)

Although the sunset is clear in this photograph, residents like Alexander Gordon of South Hero (1750–1802) tell of a "dark day" throughout the islands. Unknown to islanders at the time, forest fires spreading across Ontario on May 19, 1780, sent heavy smoke into cloudy New England skies. The result was 36 hours of inexplicable, terrifying darkness in which lanterns and candles were needed during the day. (Courtesy of Ron Fierstein.)

In the 1940s, even the smallest towns held scrap metal drives and junk rallies for collecting items to be recycled into military equipment and munitions during World War II. Tin cans, junk metal, and even rubber were all reused. Here, from left to right, Rodrick Blair, Philidore Patanode, Don Hadd, Gerald Hadd, and Harold Prarie sit proudly by a pile of collected scrap metal in Alburgh. (Courtesy of the Alburgh Historical Society.)

In 1950s North Hero, sturgeon nets were rolled on large wooden spools. Legend tells of Champ, a benevolent "sea monster" roaming Lake Champlain. Some people theorize that Champ is a huge specimen of lake sturgeon, which grow to 18 feet long. Hundreds of people have had Champ sightings. Even Samuel de Champlain claimed to have seen a "strange monster" in the waterway. (Courtesy of the Vermont State Archives and Records Administration.)

The Sand Bar State Park, across the lake from South Hero in Milton, was opened in 1933 as part of a Great Depression–era public works program. It is bordered on two sides by 1,000 acres of the Sandbar Wildlife Refuge, which offered excellent views of migratory birds and other wildlife. The public park offered an attractive lunch spot for these picnickers in 1950, as it does for thousands of visitors to this day. Over 2,000 feet of sandy beach and ample shade trees create a

relaxing day at the lakeshore. Sediment washing down from the Lamoille River runs off to create both the sandbar and the sandy beach that goes far into the lake. The wide expanse of shallow water makes this a popular beach for families with young children. (Courtesy of the Vermont State Archives and Records Administration.)

BIBLIOGRAPHY

Bellico, Russell P. *Sails and Steam in the Mountains: A Maritime and Military History of Lake George and Lake Champlain*. Fleischmanns, New York: Purple Mountain Press, 1992.

Bender, Jan. *A History of the Town of Grand Isle as Told by the People of the Town*. Grand Isle, Vermont: Landside Press, 1991.

Dale, Marty. "The Story of the Elizabeth Fisk Looms." FiskLooms, Elizabeth Fisk Looms Heritage Project. http://www.fisklooms.org/history.html.

Duffy, John, and Vincent Feeney. *Vermont: An Illustrated History*. Sun Valley, California: American Historical Press, 2000.

Liptak, Andrew. "Historical Timeline of Abnaki." The Camp Abnaki Alumni Association. http://www.oldabnaki.net/node/25.

Mumley, Steve. "Milk Train." Rutland Railroad Historical Society. http://users.rcn.com/jimdu4/MilkTrains/themilk.htm.

Perkins, George H. *Report of the State Geologist on the Mineral Industries and Geology of Vermont*. Albany: J. B. Lyon Company, 1902.

Stratton, Allen L. *History of the Town of Alburgh Vermont*. Barre, Vermont: Northlight Studio Press, 1986.

———. *History of the Town of Isle La Motte Vermont*. Barre, Vermont: Northlight Studio Press, 1984.

———. *History of the Town of North Hero Vermont*. Burlington, Vermont: George Little Press, 1976.

———. *History of the South Heroe Island Being the Towns of South Hero and Grand Isle*. Vol. 1. Burlington, Vermont: Queen City Printers, 1980.

INDEX

Visit us at
arcadiapublishing.com

www.ingramcontent.com/pod-product-compliance
Lightning Source LLC
Chambersburg PA
CBHW050644110426
42813CB00007B/1911